ARCHITECTURE IN

WOOD

WILL PRYCE

ARCHITECTURE IN
WOOD

A WORLD HISTORY

WITH OVER 400 COLOUR ILLUSTRATIONS

Thames & Hudson

FOR MY PARENTS

On the preceding pages

Page 1 Cathedral of the Transfiguration,
Kizhi Island, Russia
Page 2 Altes Rathaus, Bamberg, Germany
Page 3 Bryggen, Bergen, Norway
Page 4 Altes Rathaus, Esslingen, Germany
Page 5 Petajavesi church, Finland
Page 6 Skyrose Chapel, California, USA
Page 7 Viharn Nam Tame, Lampang, Thailand
Page 8–9 Jean-Marie Tjibaou Cultural Centre,
Noumea, New Caledonia
Page 10 Himeji Castle, Japan

First published in the United Kingdom in 2005 by
Thames & Hudson Ltd, 181A High Holborn,
London WC1V 7QX

www.thamesandhudson.com

© 2005 Thames & Hudson Ltd, London

British Library Cataloguing-in-Publication Data
A catalogue record for this book is available from the
British Library

ISBN-13: 978-0-500-34213-8
ISBN-10: 0-500-34213-X

Printed and bound in Singapore by C.S. Graphics

CONTENTS

PREFACE

Augustus the Strong (1670–1733), Elector of Saxony, articulated a common prejudice when he boasted that he had 'found Dresden small and made of wood and had left it large, splendid and made of stone'. Stone buildings, for Augustus, were self-evidently superior to wooden ones. The British art historian James Fergusson inadvertently agreed with Augustus when in 1876 he criticized Burmese monasteries for being 'built of wood – a practice… depriving them wholly of that monumental appearance of stability which is so essential to true architectural expression'. Had Fergusson been in a wooden monastery during an earthquake, however, he would have appreciated the fact that it was far more stable than a masonry building. But Fergusson was concerned with what 'looked' stable, not with structural competence, and what looked stable to him was something that was built out of stone. A.L. Castellan, the French traveller, had displayed a similar view in 1811 when he declared of Turkish yali: 'These crazy palaces with their airy architecture resemble paper châteaux built by children from cut-outs; they have no structural strength.' Over several hundred years, the yali had more than proved their structural strength but, again, their failing was that they didn't 'look' strong.

For Augustus, Fergusson and Castellan proper architecture was built with masonry. Throughout their long history, wooden buildings have been separated from the rest of architecture for failing to have the same attributes as masonry buildings. This prejudice is with us still. The 1993 edition of Brumfield's seminal *A History of Russian Architecture*, for example, has a striking photograph of a wooden building on its front cover. Wooden architecture, however, fails to warrant inclusion in the 498 pages of main text but is tacked on in a 20-page appendix at the back.

This book sets out to suggest that, far from being an inherently inferior building material, wood is simply a different one. It traces an alternative and often disregarded tradition, which predates masonry architecture but has continued to coexist with it. This parallel history features some famous but also many entirely overlooked buildings. Together they constitute a distinct architectural tradition that has its own technical logic.

This is not an exhaustive study of wooden architecture's long history; such a work would have run to many volumes. Instead it is a selection of arguably the best buildings and those most representative of important regional traditions. It is therefore, necessarily, a subjective view. It is, nonetheless, an attempt to present wooden architecture from all over the world as a coherent subject in its own right. For the purposes of this study 'wooden architecture' refers to buildings that are structurally supported by wood, rather than those that merely employ it as a cladding.

LEFT The bound timber frame
forms the basis of traditional
Kanak architecture in
New Caledonia
RIGHT The masterpiece of
blockwork architecture:
the Cathedral of the
Transfiguration, Kizhi Island,
Russia, 1714

INTRODUCTION
A WAY OF BUILDING

'Architecture' was almost certainly pioneered in wood. It provided mankind's first built shelter and techniques of jointing wood were later translated into masonry. But the fragility of wood relative to stone or brick has meant that examples of very old buildings are scarce and their influence on masonry architecture is not always easy to see.

In England, for example, the earliest monuments of Neolithic design were believed to be the stone circles at sites such as Avebury and Stonehenge. Recently, however, the invention of a technique to measure subtle variations in the soil's magnetism has demonstrated the pre-existence of older timber temples and circles and shown that a wooden temple at least twice the size of Stonehenge and 500 years older had been built at the site of a stone circle at Stanton Drew in Somerset. Further research led Alex Gibson, author of *Stonehenge and Timber Circles* (1998), to conclude that 'Stonehenge is not a stone circle… but in fact a timber circle, though unusually made in stone'.

Wooden construction served as the blueprint for many of the major masonry architectural traditions all over the world. The earliest surviving examples of Hindu architecture were cut from rock-faces in India. The shapes of these temples were derived directly from wood and bamboo construction. Cavernous ceilings were hewn out of the rock to include the shape of rafters. The carvings of lintels and doorway jambs indicate original timber joinery complete with projecting lintels. Vitruvius described the birth of classical architecture in Greece as the consequence of the replication, in stone, of the post-and-beam techniques characteristic of wooden buildings, the posts forming the basis of the classical column. The distinctive pyramidal roofs and onion domes of Russian architecture are forms invented as a direct consequence of building with horizontal logs.

It is hard now to imagine how ubiquitous wooden architecture once was. As recently as the beginning of the nineteenth century cities such as Strasbourg, Rouen and New York contained as many

wooden buildings as masonry ones; Moscow, Tokyo, Bangkok and Beijing contained far more. At this time wood was still the most popular building material in most of Central, Eastern and Northern Europe, North America, South-East Asia and Japan.

The sheer quantity of wooden buildings reflected the degree to which the planet was naturally forested. Five thousand years ago there were over 8 billion hectares (19 billion acres) of forest covering its surface; today a little over 3 million (7.5 million acres) survive. The forests that do remain, however, illustrate the type of resources once widely available.

In general, different forest species congregate in horizontal bands around the circumference of the Earth, reflecting the common climatic characteristics of particular latitudes. To the far north the boreal forests form a great ring just below the Arctic Circle. They stretch the length of northern Russia, Canada and Scandinavia, and account for one-third of the world's total forest area. Made of evergreen conifers (or 'softwoods'), these boreal forests are largely populated by members of the pine family (*pinacea*), which includes such excellent building timber as fir, pine, spruce and larch. These trees also grow in mountainous areas above 1,500m (4,921ft) such as the Alps, Carpathians, Rockies and the Kii mountains of Japan where the altitude replicates the cold climate of the far north.

Massive forests of deciduous (or 'hardwood') trees grow below the boreal ring in places such as eastern North America, Central and Eastern Europe, eastern China and lowland Japan. These areas are characterized by their cold winters, warm summers and year-round precipitation: ideal conditions for oaks, beeches, birches, maples, chestnuts, aspens and the like. In Europe and North America, the oak was the most popular source of timber.

Around the equator lie the tropical rainforests. These cover South America, Central Africa and the whole of South-East Asia all the way down to northern Australia. Average temperatures in this zone are 20–29°C (68–84°F) and annual rainfall is around 150cm (59in) of rain per year. Here the richest source of timber is not the tropical rainforest proper, for these areas contain a huge variety of different tree species. Instead, the hardwood rainforests, or 'monsoon forests', provide the best sources. These have a long dry season followed by a short monsoon and are often dominated by one or two species. Teak (*tectona grandis*), for example, predominates in Burma and northern Thailand, whereas Indonesia's forests are typically made up of members of the *dipterocarpacae* family, particularly sal.

Countries in which conifer and deciduous trees proliferated often combined both in wooden architecture. In Japan the conifers pine, cypress and fir provided the principal building members, while furniture and fixtures were typically made in hardwoods such as oak and chestnut. The most valued sources of timber were

northern Russia competence in wooden house-building was such an accepted way of life that travelling merchants carried their own tools with them with which to erect trading posts when they arrived. That said, many of the major Russian wooden churches were the work of professional master-craftsmen of exceptional skill who designed and built with equal facility.

The practice of carpentry was awarded the greatest status in Japan. Here, not only had carpenters been organized into trade guilds for centuries, but important temples housed their carpenters nearby and allowed them to bequeath their jobs. Indeed, in Japan the practice of instructing carpenters was a quasi-religious under-taking. In part this reflected the fact that the sheer complexity of Japanese wooden buildings ensured that the requisite skills could only be acquired over an extensive apprenticeship.

Most carpenters, whether amateur or professional, used two techniques of wooden construction. One employs logs placed horizontally to transfer load in 'log construction' (or 'blockwork') while the other draws primary support from the vertical placement of the tree trunk in 'frame construction'.

In blockwork tree trunks are laid horizontally on top of each other to create walls. The structure is created by erecting two adjoining walls at the same time with their logs notched at the ends to lock them together. This is done with either whole round logs (minus the bark) or by squaring off the trunk to use just the 'heartwood', the hardened core of the trunk that gives the trees structural rigidity. Prepared timbers must be interlocked at least one log's width in, in order to prevent the inherently weaker end-grain of the wood from becoming the structural support for the wall. Three types of notch are used. The basic form is a type of cradle joint in which a semicircular cut is made in either the upper or lower log in order that one should rest upon the other. Often this joint is replaced by the 'secure notch joint', in which angular notches with flat

TOP The 14th-century covered bridge of Kapellbrücke, Lucerne, Switzerland, a fragment of Western Europe's wooden past, itself damaged by fire in the 1990s
ABOVE The Burmese used round wooden columns to support their frames; the walls are thin plank infill panels

the cypresses. *Hinoki* was the most popular species of building timber, bettered only by *ma-ki*, or 'true wood', which was so admired during the Edo period (1603–1867) that its use was reserved for the most important members of the samurai class.

The kind of people who built wooden buildings varied enor-mously from culture to culture. In many societies the ability to erect wooden houses was a prerequisite of every family group, but other cultures have traditions of professional carpentry that go back millennia. In Germany, for instance, the Goths employed men called carpenters as early as AD 350; in neighbouring Austria, however, the term 'carpenter' (*Zimmermann*) was unknown in some districts until the mid-nineteenth century. Here, as in remote rural communities anywhere in the world, farmers built their own farm buildings until well into the twentieth century. In

surfaces are used to create a tighter joint under the weight of the logs. The third common solution is a 'half-dovetail joint', which allows a close interlocking fit that further pulls the logs together as the structure settles.

Frame construction, unlike blockwork or any form of masonry architecture, does not rely upon the inherent weight of the material to achieve stability. Traditionally members are attached to each other by wood joints, although today metal joints are commonly used instead. Joints work independently of gravity. As Richard Harris has observed of European timber-framing: 'a giant could pick up a timber-framed house, turn it upside down and put it back on the ground still in one piece.' Frame-construction buildings are raised in a variety of ways around the world, but all use an extrapolation of a few basic types of joints. 'Lap joints' simply overlap two thinned-down members and are then hammered through with a wooden dowel (a form of nail) to secure the joint. The more complex 'mortice-and-tenon' joint requires the cutting or drilling of a hole (the 'mortice') into which a thinner member

(the 'tenon') is placed. Finally, because tree trunks are often not as long as buildings, various types of 'scarf joint' are used to join two pieces together in a line. The most complex ways of jointing frames, however, are those devised in the Far East, particularly in Japan, where the 'bracket set' became a central part of building design. In simple terms this involves cantilevering layers of mortice-and-tenon joints into composite units, which enables a few columns to support the very heavy roofs favoured by Japanese carpenters.

Wooden frames are converted into solid walls using techniques of infilling and cladding. Infills, such as wooden boards or wattle and daub, merely fill in the gaps in the frame, while cladding systems, such as weatherboards or shingles, cover the whole structure in a protective waterproof layer. Weatherboards are formed by overlapping thin planks of wood that taper in section across the grain. These are cleft from the log radially, with the thinnest point nearest the centre of the heartwood. The placement of the thinner end at the top and the thicker at the bottom allows the boards to throw off rainwater.

ABOVE & BELOW The shingles covering the simple Hoxie House, Cape Cod, c. 1665, shown above, would later inspire the shingle style, such as at the Isaac Bell House, 1881–83, shown below

ABOVE The truncated cruciform church of Ruovesi, Finland, 1777–78, integrates blockwork walls and a framed roof to create a large open interior

Although other techniques of erecting wooden buildings have existed, none has remained in use for as long. A system of erecting upright trunks next to each other was used for centuries as a system of fortification. The vertical Saxon members of St Andrew's church at Greenstead in Essex illustrate its use in church architecture as far back as the ninth century. But this technique has only been in sporadic use. It last appeared in nineteenth-century Queensland farm buildings in Australia, where hardwood slabs were split from local timber and used vertically abutting the floor. As late as 1913 the *Queensland Agricultural Jour-* *nal* ran articles on how to construct them but they were replaced by framed buildings on hardwood stumps, which became the Queensland vernacular.

Frame and blockwork techniques have coexisted for hundreds of years in many parts of the world, and both hard- and softwoods have been used with each method. Blockwork, however, has only predominated in countries with dense forests of conifers with regular trunks. Since the trunks of hardwoods grow in widely varying sizes of cross section they have to be worked into timbers prior to use in either system. These trees,

ABOVE Church of the Archangel Michael, Lake Onega, Russia

which grow less densely and more slowly, can be used as thin wooden frame members because of their greater strength.

Wood performs well as a building material in widely differing climates. It is an excellent insulator and blockwork buildings in both Scandinavia and Russia have made the bitter winter climate tolerable. In 1591 the British diplomat Giles Fletcher noted the suitability of Russia's wooden houses: 'This [wooden] building seemeth far better for their country than that of stone and brick, as being colder and more dampish than their wooden houses, specially of fir that is a dry and warm wood.'

Wood has also been used to construct light, open and airy structures that combat the heat and humidity of South-East Asia. Wood has a very high strength-to-weight ratio. Spruce and pine, for example, can provide the same degree of strength with a structure 16 times lighter than steel and five times lighter than concrete. Because of its light weight the wooden frame has allowed houses to be carried around in response to the changing lives of their occupants. When individuals married or died their houses could be reused either whole or in part in other locations. In addition, in the Far East, Indonesia and the western coast of North America the inherent flexibility of the wooden frame has allowed it to withstand earthquakes in a way that masonry architecture, reliant for stability on its inherent weight, has never been able to.

CHAPTER ONE
THE FAR EAST

The wooden architecture of the Far East is instantly recognizable. Its distinctive character results from the total absence of any discernible cross-bracing members. Truss technology was certainly understood but deliberately ignored in favour of a sophisticated frame system which originated in China but which was quickly disseminated to Korea and Japan. In this system the prime consideration is the support of an enormous roof, the walls being merely infilling panels. The roof was supported by a complex maze of mortice-and-tenon joints grouped in 'bracket sets' whose members reach out like a candelabra to support a range of horizontal beams above. These sets enabled individual columns to support much greater loads than would otherwise have been possible. Very heavy roofs protected the buildings against the constant barrage of seismic activity. The fact that the vast majority of historic architecture is wooden, and some of it over a thousand years old, is testimony to the success of the bracket-

set frame in withstanding earthquakes. Using horizontal beams (purlins) as the primary element of the roof structure has also enabled craftsmen to adjust their roof profiles to any particular shape, hence allowing the beautiful curved roofs so characteristic of the region.

Buddhism has also been of seminal importance. But it seems that for a long period of time a huge degree of cultural cross-fertilization took place between China, Korea and Japan in isolation from neighbouring states. Only in the eighteenth century did the influence of this architecture really reach Western civilization, but then its impact was immediately noticeable.

History has been particularly cruel to Korean architecture and a huge number of important historical structures have had to be rebuilt. As a consequence this chapter looks at examples located solely in Japan and China, although Korea's influence is clearly visible in the architecture of Japan.

China's vegetation is broadly split between a highly forested

eastern half and a vast dry interior. It is almost unique in that the eastern woodlands extend in an unbroken expanse of continuous forest from the tropical forest in the south to the boreal forest on the Russian border. It can roughly be divided into a handful of forest types which form broad latitudinal bands across the country: rainforest, evergreen broad-leafed forest, mixed mesophytic forest, temperate deciduous forest and finally boreal coniferous forest. Because of China's long history as an integrated state the emperors have had access to

a vast choice of timber for their major projects. While many such projects have been destroyed, the imperial complexes of the Temple of Heaven and Forbidden City illustrate much of what is unique about the way the Chinese view wood. Unfortunately their constituent structures have had to be replaced relatively recently. Only in Japan do examples of wooden architecture remain from a range of historical periods. Here virtually all historic architecture is timber-framed, joined together by intricate bracket sets, which provide great strength and

flexibility. This has allowed the wooden buildings to withstand Japan's incessant earthquakes, some of them since the seventh century AD. Their remarkable survival also provides much of our knowledge of early Chinese and Korean wooden architecture, which has long since been destroyed.

Japanese expertise with wood seems to reflect a philosophical affinity as much as a practical need. Japan's indigenous religion, Shintoism, is an animist faith which ascribes conscious will to natural forces such as the wind and rain, sun and

moon, and to natural features such as mountains and forests. Without the permission and assistance of those spirits, the cycles of human life would be jeopardized; crops would not grow and women would not conceive.

Trees, like other organisms, are believed to possess spirits, and a carpenter, when he cuts down a tree, assumes a moral responsibility as the spirit remains in the timber. To this day traditional carpenters still vow before they fell a tree to continue its existence. The weight of this responsibility also ensured that

FAR LEFT The Phoenix Hall of the Byodo-in, near Uji, Japan, 1053
LEFT 'Nigatsu-do' (or 'February Hall'), sub-temple of Todai-ji, Nara, Japan, supplies water for spiritual purification

in Japan building in wood was a special way of life. The carpenter's significance is indicated by the Japanese *daiku*, which literally means 'great builder' or 'great craftsman'.

The Japanese islands have a temperate but humid climate and a mountainous topography ideal for the growth of a range of softwoods such as cedar, pine, cypress and fir and deciduous trees such as oak and chestnut. The wood they prized above all others was *hinoki* (Japanese cypress). This conifer can grow over 40m (130ft) tall, with a fine, straight grain. Its timber is strong, resilient and remarkably resistant to warping. It was almost universally employed from the sixth up to the thirteenth century, when supplies became depleted. From then on, builders substituted red pine (*akamatsu*) or the cheaper black pine (*kuromatsu*) or Japanese chestnut (*tochi*).

Despite the reverence afforded to Japan's natural heritage, Japanese architecture is not a direct response to the islands' climate. Rather it was the arrival and assimilation of the Buddhist faith from India via China and Korea that stimulated the great wooden architecture of Japan. And this involved the introduction of an essentially subtropical building style, which was never really modified to reflect Japan's much colder climate. Throughout, comfort has been sacrificed to simplicity.

Architecture has also always had a subtle relationship with political control in Japan. The emperors who first founded Nara and then Kyoto were known as the *mikado*, literally 'honourable gateway'. Temple complexes used Buddhist teaching to emphasize the spiritual significance of the emperor in

emulation of the emperors of China. In return the first monastery complexes were designed as enormous monuments, as in
Todai-ji in Nara. When the monks were perceived as wielding
too much power, the capital was moved in AD 794 to Heian-
kyo (present-day Kyoto) and new monasteries were planned to
emulate the scale of domestic buildings rather than those of
the emperor. Here the central temple complexes of To-ji and
Nishi-Hongan-ji illustrate this revised scale. As power shifted
to the shoguns, powerful individuals known as the *kenmon*, or
'gateway of power', the castle and palace architecture they

built reflected the changing pattern of authority. But throughout, the relative political stability of Japan has allowed for
the survival of historic structures from periods denuded of
wooden buildings elsewhere in the world.

**ABOVE The Pavilion to Usher
in Light (Yan Hui Ge) in the
Imperial Gardens of the
Forbidden City, Beijing, China
OVERLEAF This sculpture
mandala in the *kodo* of To-ji,
Kyoto, Japan, consists of 21
major sculptures from the 9th
century, commissioned by the
esoteric Buddhist leader Kukai,
who founded the temple**

HORU-JI

Buddhism was introduced to Japan in 552 by the first in a succession of monks from China and later Korea. Once the royal family had been converted, they built a series of foundations, which followed the Chinese model of the monastery temple. These complexes were derived from secular and religious architecture in China, which they closely resemble. Consisting of courtyards enclosing a series of wooden buildings standing on masonry plinths, they are laid out symmetrically, orientated south.

In 607 the Empress Suiko (r. 593–628) and the regent Shotoku Taishi founded Horu Temple (Horu-ji) about 20km (32 miles) from the capital Fujiwara. Although it was burnt down in 670, parts of the rebuilt version survive to this day. Here the five-storey pagoda, the Golden Hall (*kondo*), the Inner Gate (*chumon*) and most of the surrounding corridor (*kaino*) are the oldest wooden buildings in the world.

The very oldest is the Golden Hall, which dates from 677 and was built to house images of the Buddha. The structure is supported by round pillars with entasis revealing a profile reminiscent of classical Greece. These hold 'cloud brackets' (*kumo hijiki*) whose profiles resemble clouds. Also below the bressummer beam of the upper storey is a type of strut that is a primitive form of the characteristic 'frog crotch' (*kaeru-meta*). Both these details appear on the rock carvings of the Tat'ung caves in Shanxi province in China and indicate the North Wei style of architecture, itself derived from the fifth-century Gupta era in India.

Beside the Golden Hall stands the pagoda in which symbolic relics of the Buddha were enshrined. The pagoda form clearly derives originally from the spires of Indian stupas. This type of structure is strengthened by a single wooden column,

called the *shinbashira* or 'heart pillar', which runs down its centre from the spire to the ground, where it rests on a foundation. Below it are interred relics representing the bones of the Buddha. As such the pagoda serves as a symbol of the sanctity of the precinct.

During the eighth century pagodas declined in importance in temple design. At Horu-ji the pagoda shares the same axis as the Golden Hall but at Yukushi-ji, erected in the 720s, the pagoda has been moved off this axis. According to the Chinese laws of composition, this meant doubling it to flank the pre-eminent Golden Hall. One survives to this day and is unique among Japanese pagodas for having double eaves on its storey, giving its profile the definite rhythm famously described by American art historian Ernest Fenella as 'frozen music'.

BOTTOM LEFT Eastern pagoda, Yakushi-ji. Originally built in the late 7th century, then rebuilt in the AD 720s, this remarkable *mokoshi*, a lean-to component attached to each of the three levels, means that the pagoda appears to have six storeys
ABOVE LEFT Golden Hall (*kondo*), Horu-ji, AD 677

ABOVE A freestanding belfry just outside Horu-ji's eastern precinct
TOP The Horu-ji precinct. The five-storey pagoda, Inner Gate (*chumon*) and most of the surrounding corridor (*kaino*) are among the oldest wooden buildings in the world

NARA AND TODAI-JI

In 708 the Empress Genmei chose to move the royal court from Fujiwara some 20km (32 miles) to the south to Heijo (now known as Nara). In the years that followed, an impressive building campaign supported by an expanding government bureaucracy created an entirely new city.

A whole government department, the Construction Bureau (Mokuryo), was established in 728 to oversee temple and public-building construction in accordance with the new city plan. A separate ministry was then created to supervise the building of the Heijo Palace, an enormous compound over ⅓ mile (1km) square, containing government buildings and the emperor's residence.

The emperors may have personally embraced the Buddhist faith but its adoption had consequences far beyond mere choice of worship. Buddhist texts were replete with extensive lists of the benefits that awaited the generous temporal sponsor. Rulers were promised dynastic stability, political calm and prosperity in return for their patronage. When, in 740, the Emperor Shomu decreed that every Japanese province should build a monastery, to be called a Realm-Guarding Temple, he was proclaiming himself the servant of the three treasures of Japan: the Buddha, Buddhist Law and the monastic community.

Shomu's masterpiece was the creation of the monastery complex of Todai-ji in 745. This was designed to administer all the others. The department responsible for its construction employed 227 site supervisors, 917 master builders and 1,483 labourers. The master plan involved a series of great buildings on a north–south axis eventually to be flanked by two colossal seven-storey pagodas. At its apex was the casting of a bronze Great Buddha and, to house it, the largest building ever to have been made of wood, the Great Buddha Hall (Daibutsuden),

was constructed. Twice burnt down by invading armies in the twelfth and sixteenth centuries, the current Great Buddha Hall is only two-thirds its original size, but it remains the largest wooden building in the world. The scale of ambition at Todai-ji can still be sensed today. Among the motives of its creators must have been the desire to construct a fitting centrepiece for a city to rival the legendary Chinese T'ang capital of Chang'an (now Xi'an).

TOP The Hokkedo is the oldest structure at Todai-ji, built in the AD 730s and remodelled in the 12th century. The original single-shell technique of the roof has been retained and shows the mature T'ang style from China
ABOVE Sculptures from the Great Buddha Hall (Daibutsuden), Todai-ji
FAR LEFT The Nigatsu-do sub-temple of Todai-ji has panoramic views over over the Yamato Plain

ABOVE The Hokkedo seen from the direction of the Great Buddha Hall, Todai-ji

LEFT The Great Buddha Hall (Daibutsuden) was burnt down in the 12th and 16th centuries. While now only two-thirds its original size, it is still the largest wooden building in the world

U J I
THE PURE LAND

The year 1051 was of particular significance to Buddhist Japan. It was widely believed to be the 1,500th anniversary of the death of the Buddha and would mark the end of the protection of his teaching. This impression was reinforced by a plague epidemic that raged in the capital. The following year one of Japan's holiest temples, the Hasedera, burnt down. The name of the era itself was changed in the hope of averting further suffering. Perhaps Buddhism's end as predicted by the Buddha had come. This would halt the perpetual cycle of death and life, much like turning off the music in musical chairs.

One possibility of escape seemed to lie in the legend of a monk named Dharmakara who had vowed that, upon his attaining Buddhahood, all who believed in him and called his name would be born into a paradise where they could await enlightenment. Dharmakara became the Amida Buddha, worshipped by the 'Pure Land' sect who taught a form of religious devotion aimed not at immediate enlightenment in the present life but in rebirth in the Amida Buddha's 'Pure Land'. Consequently court nobles built private Buddha Halls on their country estates in order to keep an Amida figure close at hand in anticipation of their own demise, and it is one of these halls that is the surviving glory of Heian period architecture (784–1185).

The Phoenix Hall (Hoodo) of the Byodo-in near Uji was built by Yorimichi, head of the Fujiwara family, in 1053 as an addition to his father's villa. This beautifully proportioned structure is a highly original design. It was not modelled on earlier temple structures nor did it resemble other Buddha Halls. Yorimichi's invention has been described as resembling a stylized phoenix with wing-like flanking aisles and a tail aisle to the rear. It forms a shallow U shape and sits on an island in a lake facing eastwards, in the direction of the Uji River.

It is one of the very few buildings from medieval Japan to have been copied exactly, and where the derivative buildings were described as such in contemporary sources. It was immediately considered to have set a new standard of architectural perfection. It is also unusual in having been largely designed for contemplation from its exterior alone. The central chapel, which houses the Amida figure, has both hip-and-gable and lower skirt roofs, which give it the appearance of two storeys, when in fact it has only one. Likewise, the side aisles have upper storeys of such squatness as to be impractical. Most importantly of all, in certain light conditions, the Amida figure can be half-descried through a latticework screen from across the water. Here excavations reveal that a viewing structure, the Little Palace, was built to shelter penitents while they worshipped from the opposite bank.

The Phoenix Hall is both a temple and the altar itself. Literally aping the Chinese symbol of rebirth, the phoenix, it also provides a dazzling evocation of the serene beauties of Amida's paradise. As Yorimachi's descendant Tadazane (1078–1162) exclaimed on first seeing it in 1118, 'It is marvellous, a veritable imitation of the Pure Land.' This was a reaction that had been carefully engineered.

ABOVE The Phoenix Hall (Hoodo) of the Byodo-in, near Uji, 1053. Miniature 'turrets' adorn the corners, a feature probably derived from Chinese palaces
BELOW The hall's delicate members have had to survive considerable neglect since it was built
LEFT One of two phoenixes on the roofline of the Phoenix Hall. But its name actually derives from its stylized plan
OVERLEAF The Phoenix Hall was designed to be contemplated from the opposite bank, its aisles stretched out like wings on either side

NARA

THE 'INDIAN STYLE'

The Heian period came to an end in the Gempei War (1180–85), which resulted in victory for the Minamoto warrior clan and the imperial appointment of Minamoto no Yoritomo as shogun. From now on, the emperor would reign from Kyoto but Yoritomo in Kamakura would exercise real power.

One of the casualties of the war was the great monastery temple of Todai-ji whose monks had supported Yoritomo. The shogun ordered its reconstruction under the direction of the great prelate Shunjobo Chogen. Chogen had been to China three times in pursuit of Buddhist teaching and culture. He employed the Chinese Ch'en brothers to direct the recasting of the Great Buddha. It was probably in discussion with them that his ambitious scheme for the rebuilding of the temple was first formulated.

The result is what is known as the 'Indian style' (or sometimes the 'Daibutsuden style'), but its origins probably lay in Sung China. The most radical feature of this style was its system of bracketing. The main columns rose all the way to the upper roof as the multiple tiers of brackets attach through

them and are stabilized by lateral members extending the length of the building. This demanded trees of prodigious height to provide the columns. Those of the Great South Gate (Nandeimon) reach 20m (65ft), those of the lost Great Buddha Hall (Daibutsuden) half as high again.

Chogen and the Ch'ens explored the mountains of Suo province in search of the giant trees required. They may well have been aided in their quest by an influential contemporary carpentry tool. The twelfth century saw the invention and widespread use of the carpenter's square. This used a square root of scale and a simple right angle to profound effect. It enabled workmen to calculate the dimensions of the square member that could be cut from a round log.

What is certain is that the Indian style employed many members of the same size of section, enabling them to be easily mass-produced. However, once they had been found and felled, the logistics of returning the trees to Nara were complex. First, they were transported through a network of rivers and across the Inland Sea. The final overland section of the journey

required an enormous effort. The logs were hauled in great wagons, each drawn by 120 oxen and devotees who wished to gain merit by the endeavour. The latter team included, albeit only nominally, the retired emperor Shirakura II and his court.

The Great South Gate of Todai-ji was completed in 1199 and is the most important part of Chogen's reconstruction to survive to this day. The huge pillars which are visible right up to their tops are each a single massive tree trunk. Surmounting them are great capitals, on which rest the crossbeams which are themselves surmounted by the tie beams that support the pitch of the roof.

Lower down no fewer than 19 brackets are mortised right through the pillars to support the deep eaves of upper and lower roofs. They are balanced by extending seven brackets into tie beams, which span the entire structure. Big wedges inserted at the corners above the purlins give the eaves their characteristic strong curves.

This profile was repeated a generation later in the Todai-ji belfry built by Chogen's successor Eisai. This structure has an Indian-style feel, with its thick frame employed on a large scale for a one-storey, one-bay building. Huge studs support the tie beams, with transverse beams placed directly on top. An enormous bell hangs from the centre of the beams. However, the comparatively simple four-step bracket and block system below the eaves resembles the new 'Zen style', a fresh Chinese import which was to replace the Indian style almost immediately.

Chogen's death in 1195 may have been the deciding factor in the swift disappearance of the Indian style, or it may have been its unfortunate association with an increasingly unpopular shogunate. But perhaps it is simply that its severity did not really appeal to Japanese tastes.

KYOTO

THE GOLDEN AND SILVER PAVILIONS

In 1338, immediately after the collapse of the first Minamoto shogunate, the Ashikaga family established a second military government. It retained power for over 200 years, a span now described as the Muromachi period.

One of the finest Muromachi designs to survive is the Golden Pavilion (Kinkaku-ji), originally erected in 1398 for the third Ashikaga shogun, Yoshimitsu. This is a pavilion conceived as a compositional element in the landscaped gardens of a villa which lay to the north-east of Kyoto. It is part Zen temple, part contemplative pavilion, and its varied lineage is visible in its mix of architectural styles. The square lantern top storey, with its curving pyramidal roof, looks Chinese. The delicacy of the details, the visible framing and shingled roof are all very definitely Japanese.

The ground floor contains the Chamber of Dharma Water (Hosuiin). It is walled with reticulated shutters and links to a small kiosk standing over the water. The first floor, containing the Tower of the Sound of Waves (Choonkaku), has sliding wooden doors and flat plank walls. It is supported by transverse arms in the Indian style. The final storey, the Cupola of the Ultimate (Kukyocho), features a formal set of Zen motifs.

The door leaves are richly panelled and the windows topped by a cusped arch.

In 1484 the eighth Ashikaga shogun, Yoshimasa, began to build a villa in Kyoto's eastern hills. Its Silver Pavilion (Ginkaku-ji) was still unfinished when he died in 1490. It was converted into a temple to his memory. A small structure with a ground floor only 7 by 5.5m (23 by 18ft), it contains the Hall of Emptied Mind (Shinkuden) and its features derive from a residential style, the Shoin Zukuri ('Book Hall' or 'Study Construction'). This indicates the changes in residential design in the intervening century. The large central room plan was replaced by a series of modular spaces. These were defined by paper and wood composite panels instead of shuttered screens. Porches on both floors afford views of the surrounding pool and gardens.

It is believed that Yoshimasa intended to cover the building with silver leaf as a foil to his forebear's pavilion. He certainly duplicated its cypress-bark pyramidal roof surmounted by a phoenix.

ABOVE The Golden Pavilion (Kinkaku-ji), Kyoto, was erected in 1398 but destroyed by arson in 1950. It was rebuilt in 1955 with an extraordinary degree of exactitude
RIGHT Detail of the eaves, Golden Pavilion
OVERLEAF The Silver Pavilion (Ginkaku-ji), Kyoto, finished after 1490, epitomizes the refinement of late-medieval Japanese taste

FROM CASTLE TO PALACE

The Momoyama period (1573–1615) was a time of intense military activity during which Japan became unified under a single leader. Castle architecture became supremely important, both as a means of enforcing military rule and of providing it with a potent symbol of authority.

During the late sixteenth and early seventeenth centuries, when castle building was at its peak, over one hundred castles were built in Japan. Many were constructed on a scale and with a degree of technical sophistication equal to the finest European fortifications. Yet unlike European fortresses, they used not only stone defences but also colossal wooden frames designed to withstand prolonged assault.

The finest extant example of Japan's unique form of castle construction is the complex of Himeji Castle (Himeji-jo), the archetypal *hirayamajiro*, or 'castle on a hill on a plain'. Himeji Castle was built after shogun Tokugawa Ieyasu gave the area to his son-in-law Ikeda Terumasa in recognition of his services at the Battle of Sekigahara. The latter constructed the castle

between 1601 and 1609 on a huge scale. The outermost of three moats enclosed most of the town of Himeji. The middle moat divided the samurai quarters off from those of the footsoldiers and townspeople. Within the inner moat a labyrinthine plan contained a sequence of gateways and gatehouses leading up a steep climb. This had to be navigated in an irregular spiral, while all the time being funnelled into progressively narrower spaces.

The complex is guarded by three towers (*tenshu*) linked to the central keep or 'guardian of the sky' (*tenshukaku*) whose plan follows the contours of the hill. The surrounding walls are topped with corridors two storeys high and armoured on both sides in order to concentrate fire on any intruder who might have reached the walls of the keep.

The keep is itself intimidating. It rises 31.5m (103ft) from its stone base, a full 100m (328ft) from the plain below. It is based on the older watchtower (*boro*) design of three independent but connected parts. Above the stone base is a two-storey section, then a middle storey out of which rises a three-storey tower.

LEFT The keep or 'guardian of the sky' (*tenshukaku*) of Himeji Castle, Kansai, 1601–09, rises 31.5m (103ft) from its stone base
ABOVE The entranceway into the castle

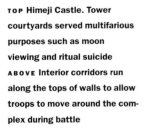 **TOP** Himeji Castle. Tower courtyards served multifarious purposes such as moon viewing and ritual suicide **ABOVE** Interior corridors run along the tops of walls to allow troops to move around the complex during battle

The entire frame is reinforced against bombardments or earthquakes by two huge pillars running from the basement to the top storey. Originally the east pillar was a single trunk of silver fir (*momi*) some 24.8m (81ft) long. The west pillar was formed by tenoning together two tree trunks, one of hemlock (*tsuga*), the other of silver fir. The design of the structure shows an astonishing comprehension of the mechanical principles governing tall structures and uses remarkably strong joints to transfer the massive loads. Possibly the builders inherited this expertise from the design of multi-storey pagodas.

Although Himeji was never tested by war, it was clearly a formidable military proposition. But it was also a self-consciously expressive and flamboyant castle design. The three towers surrounding the central keep display a different roofline over each façade, employing a range of styles including Chinese, dormer and hip-and-gable. There are cusped gables and gable ornaments, decorative bell-shaped windows overlook the residential areas, and a single exposed decorative pillar appears on the sixth storey of the keep. Defensive wall openings were rectangular for archers, with gunmen being given the option

of circles, triangles and squares. The entire complex is covered with white plaster up to the eaves. This picturesque white palette gives the castle the appearance of a great bird spreading its wings for flight, hence its alternative name, Shirasagijo, or 'White Heron Castle'.

The mounting scale of castle projects had implications, in turn, for the technology of timber construction. The two-man frame saw was both labour-intensive and difficult to forge because of the length of its blade. In response, Kyoto sawyers pioneered the production of a new one-man ripsaw, the *maekiki-oga*. This used large raked teeth on a much shorter blade to cut wood accurately and swiftly.

The same period saw the introduction of a push plane from China, which was converted into a block pull plane in Japan. It rapidly replaced the adze and planing knife for smoothing surfaces of wood. It was both faster and required a lesser degree of skill. It also led to the invention of grooving and gouging planes, which made it much easier to make multiple sliding tracks and housing for screens. This encouraged the use of more flexible interior spaces.

ABOVE The narrowing entrance corridor was overlooked by the keep. It had to be navigated by an irregular spiral overlooked by arrow and rifle holes
OVERLEAF Two huge wooden columns running up from the foundations to the roof support Himeji's lofty keep

Nijo Castle was built between 1602 and 1604 as the Kyoto residence of shogun Tokugawa Ieyasu. In 1625 and 1626, he enlarged it by adding three structures brought from Fushimi Castle. These formed the Ninomaru Palace in the centre of the complex, a visual symbol of wealth and power.

The three buildings were added to and linked with free-flowing corridors in a style now known as the *shoin-zukuri*, the style of the Japanese house. The formal progression of the visitor through a series of spaces was used to emphasize the court's position at the centre of power. The first room entered was the *tozamurai*, which contained samurai retainers; then the *shikidai*, where guests were initially received before being invited into the *ohiroma* for formal audiences with the shogun. Here status is subtly reinforced in spatial terms. The visitor arrives in the anteroom (*geden no ma*), a step below the height of the upper area (*jodan no ma*) where the shogun would sit. Two further rooms beyond housed the Kuroshoi for more private interviews with selected guests. The final chamber, the *shiro shoin*, was reserved for the master's personal use.

All the rooms are broadly square in plan and laid out on an extended stagger completely surrounded by corridors whose carpentry contains a security device. Their special 'nightingale floor' was designed to squeak when trodden on, alerting the inhabitants to unwanted visitors at night: this was made possible by the most exact timber planing together with the placing of carefully bevelled splines under the board junctions.

The Ninomaru Palace is secluded in a courtyard whose elaborate gate signified the importance of the resident. In fact,

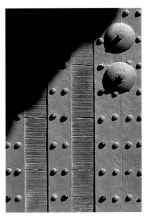

many Japanese titles derive from the symbolic values of the gate. *Mom-in* ('Dowager Empress') means literally the 'Retired One of the Palace Gate', and 'a noble family' is described using the word *meimom*, literally 'a gate of repute'. During the consolidation of Tokugawa rule military engineering was replaced by more subtle displays of power. However, the inherently political nature of architecture remained the same.

LEFT The entrance gate is of *karamon* or 'Chinese Gate' style. Its sixteen-petal chrysanthemum decoration was added when it was later taken over by the imperial household

KYOTO
EASTERN TEMPLES

The end of the great civil wars brought relative prosperity to Japan and a growth in the popularity of pilgrimage temples. These were rebuilt or extended on an increasingly lavish scale. The Main Hall (Hondo) of Kiyomizudera, which houses the principal image, was rebuilt in 1635 and is a full 33.46 by 32.18m (110 by 105ft) in plan. It is an exceptionally dramatic design, the apogee of the 'hanging construction' (*kakezukuri*) type of structure. It features a huge dancing stage, *butai*, which is flanked by two wings that run down the width of the building and are called bandstands (*gaku-ya*). Presumably created for the presentation of ceremonial dances, the entire edifice is held up by enormous posts secured by a network of tie beams overhanging a steep hillside. Above this, the whole structure is covered by a massive roof of Japanese cypress (*hinoki*) shingles.

Another of the major pilgrimage temples in Kyoto's eastern hills was the great Zen temple Nanzen-ji (South Temple of Enlightenment), the central seat of the Rinzai branch of the Zen sect. Like many of Kyoto's temples, this was originally the villa of a retired emperor, converted in 1290. By 1334 its importance was such that the Emperor Go-Daigo proclaimed it to be first among the five Zen temples.

Now it is approached by an enormous three-storey 'Gate-less Gate' (*sanmon*) of Zen scripture, which was rebuilt in 1626. Further on is the Seiryo-den, built by the Emperor Go-Yozei (1587–1611).

LEFT The wealth of the Eastern Temples can be seen in the size and adornment of their Great South Gates

LEFT Kiyomizudera's Oku-no-in (Innermost Temple) is dedicated to Kannon, the Bodhisattva ('Buddha-to-be') of infinite compassion and mercy, hence depicted with 11 faces and 'a thousand' arms

ABOVE The Main Hall (Hondo) of Kiyomizudera was rebuilt in 1635. It overlooks the city of Kyoto

THE TEMPLE OF HEAVEN

Chinese civilization is remarkable not only for its extraordinary longevity but also for its philosophical continuity. Of crucial importance was the contribution of China's most influential thinker, Confucius (551–479 BC), whose conception of moral and political order underpinned the whole of Chinese philosophy right up until the twentieth century. His vision of an ideal society was one where human beings sought to live in harmony by respecting the hierarchical balance of the universe both in relation to each other and to the state. For Confucius, filial piety should be the cornerstone of a system of relationships which saw individuals respect the wider family of man and the political structure through which that family was governed. His follower Mencius (370–300 BC) would add a significant caveat. He reminded rulers that, while they ruled with the direct mandate of heaven, they were not themselves divine, but rather were blessed with the role of intermediary between the affairs of gods and men.

Less than a century later the centralized bureaucratic monarchy, which was to dominate Chinese history, was established in the Qin dynasty (221–206 BC) and strengthened by its successors, the Han (206 BC–AD 220). During this period, China's geographical borders were defined and uniformity imposed upon its administration. The Han declared that henceforth the maintenance of local currencies, writing scripts or systems of measurement would be treasonable offences.

Han Confucians thought the natural world was comprised of five constituent elements or 'phases': fire, water, earth, metal and wood. These were governed by cyclical flows of the invisible heavenly forces of *yin* and *yang*. These words, which literally distinguish the 'dark side' from the 'light side' of a hill, were used to describe the opposing forces that kept the universe in balance. Thus historical cycles, such as battles for dynastic succession, which seemed to contradict the presence of supernatural interference, could instead be seen as reflecting the natural shifting of heavenly favour determined by a particular balance of *yin* and *yang* at the time in question. While rulers ruled well they did not disturb the balance of heaven and earth within which their position was so pivotal. Misrule might cause floods, earthquakes and plagues, but also risked the ruler being forsaken by heaven's favour and consequently replaced. Thus the Han Confucians created a philosophical system that accommodated political strife while enabling the victors to inherit not

FAR LEFT The pavilion called Prayer for a Prosperous New Year (Qinian Dian) is the largest structure in the Temple of Heaven' (Tian Tan) complex. Originally built in the early 15th century, it was rebuilt both in 1751 and 1889 after being damaged by lightning

ABOVE LEFT The roof of the circular Imperial Vault of Heaven (Huangqiongyu) pavilion

ABOVE RIGHT Both pavilions are laid out on axis with the 'altar of heaven', the platform where the emperor made offerings on the behalf of his people

only a great empire, but with it the mandate of heaven to rule.

However, the Chinese notion of 'heaven' was in no way similar to the Hellenic or Hebrew realm of Western European thought, which was ruled over by an omnipotent creator upon whom human beings were themselves modelled. It was rather an animate, but entirely abstract, cosmic force. Unlike the medieval Christian tradition, whose Great Chain of Being positioned man above the natural world, Chinese philosophy saw man as inexorably embedded within nature, with responsibilities to maintain its balance. Mountains, lakes and forests had spirits – forces which man must respect. Wood, as one of the five 'phases', was far more than a convenient building material. It was used to design buildings that would safely embed human beings within this cosmically charged landscape. The form and plan of buildings were correspondingly designed to conform with auspicious positions within the forces of *yin* and *yang*. This was done by orienting buildings in relation to the natural topography and the supernatural forces that lay within it.

The most explicit example of the symbolic nature of Chinese architecture is the Temple of Heaven (Tian Tan), which was built in 1420 shortly after the refoundation of Beijing as the imperial capital city during the Ming dynasty of 1368–1644. When the Ming came to power, the emperors controlled a vast and complex state. When the founder Taizu's fourth son, Chengzu, usurped the throne from his nephew, he moved the court from the existing capital, Nanjing, to his power base in Beijing. An entirely new imperial city was built. An important part of this was the creation of a place where, in accordance with centuries of custom, the emperor could intercede on behalf of his people and make sacrifices to the gods. The Temple of Heaven was designed as a vast walled enclosure of 273 hectares

(682 acres). At the north end it is circular to represent heaven (the circle), and at the south it is square to represent the earth.

The main ceremonial buildings and the altar line a ceremonial route down the centre of the complex. The altar is simply a round raised stone platform where the ceremony would take place. A circular walled pavilion, the Imperial Vault of Heaven (Huangqiongyu), was built to house the ceremonial tablets used in the ceremony. The current structure dates from the sixteenth century. It is supported by two timber rings resting on eight columns apiece. The outer ring supports the eaves, the inner ring supports three tiers of circular ceilings. The supporting purlins also provide the springing-off points for layers of straight eaves, which make up the concave roof shape.

Further down the ceremonial route is the Prayer for a Prosperous New Year (Qinian Dian), which is also circular in plan but is a larger triple-eaved structure. Every element in its composition has been judiciously chosen for its symbolic meaning. The roofs are painted blue to represent the sky. The 12 outer columns enclosed in the walls of the building support the lowest roof layer, and are symbolic of the 12 months of the year. The inner ring is supported by 12 columns, which run around the inside of the single enclosed space representing the 12 hours of the day (the ancient Chinese day was split into 12 rather

than 24 units). Each column is a huge piece of timber, some of which came from the forests of Yumen in south-west China, others from the USA during the rebuilding of 1890–96. The four innermost columns, which support the final roof, represent the four seasons of the year and reach 19m (62ft) from the ground. The 28 columns that support the roof represent the 28 constellations of stars worshipped by the emperor during the sacrifice to heaven.

The building is therefore designed to represent a correspondence between the earth, the emperor (representing mankind) and the universe. This relationship is symbolized by the fact that the building has three roofs and, like the altar itself, rests on three terraces accessed by three imperial carriageways of steps.

ABOVE All the buildings in the Temple of Heaven are built on a strict symmetrical axis

BEIJING
THE FORBIDDEN CITY

Imperial architecture continued to express the emperor's symbolic importance beyond the design of purely ceremonial buildings like the Temple of Heaven. The planning of the entire city of Beijing reflected the belief that it was possible to literally align the social order with the forces of heaven, and consequently improve the fortunes of its inhabitants. Thus the city was designed as a series of nested boxes. The Outer City surrounded and enclosed the Inner City. The Inner City in turn enclosed the Government District (or Imperial City), which enclosed at its heart the fortified palace compound known as the Forbidden City (Zi Jin Cheng).

The name itself is both a symbolic and practical description. 'Zi' refers to the Zi Wei star, the pole star and home of the Supreme Deity. It was located at the apex of the vault of heaven; all other stars with their respective deities revolved around it in homage. The emperor who ruled earth with heaven's mandate occupied an analogous position, residing at the apex of Beijing (and hence China). Ordinary citizens were never allowed into the Forbidden City and many of his own courtiers would never see him. The emperor was carried around the palace compound in an enclosed sedan chair and on state occasions sat behind a screen among clouds of incense.

Around him the layout of the Forbidden City was designed to reflect the harmony of the heavens. As with the Imperial City around it, it was strictly symmetrical, laid out on a north–south

axis, apart from small residential sectors to the north-east and north-west. The Outer Court contained the major ceremonial buildings, built on an axial pathway. They are odd in number, signifying *yang*, and constructed in ascending order of scale and magnificence. The Inner Court originally had two state and six residential palaces, signifying *yin*.

The complex was designed as a complete philosophical expression of state by senior court officials of the board of works, who handed over only detailed design work to master craftsmen who were at this time, at best, semi-literate. Building work took only three years, from 1417 to 1420, carried out by one million workers managed by 100,000 planners and craftsmen recruited

from all over China. But the colossal quantities of wood must have been ordered beforehand. Only nanmu (phoebe nanmu) was used, a hardwood of exceptional quality, which grew in the south-west province of Sichaun some 1,500km (900 miles) from Beijing. Its collection was a significant logistical achievement. Once felled, logs were rolled into dry mountain gullies, lashed together to form rafts and left for the rainy season torrents to plunge them down the side of the mountain. They were then transported via the Tonghui River and Imperial Grand Canal to Beijing, a journey which took three to four years. Because of its quality and importance, the wood was known as *shan mu* ('sacred timber') and stored at the Sacred Timber Yard in Beijing.

The Forbidden City was badly damaged by fires in the fifteenth and sixteenth centuries and many of its extant buildings date from the early seventeenth. During this period, craftsmen began to assume greater importance in the design process. Instrumental in this change of status were the Lei family, who had been carpenters in Nanjing from the fourteenth century. In the 1660s, during the early years of Emperor Kangxi's reign, two Lei brothers, Lei Fada and Lei Faxuan, were recruited to help reconstruct the Hall of Supreme Harmony, the centrepiece of the Outer Court. Traditionally, when the ridge beam was installed, a ritual would take place. As it was the seat of sovereign power, this was presided over by the emperor himself. During the

FAR LEFT Detail showing the column-and-beam structure inside the Hall of Supreme Harmony

ABOVE The complex public buildings were arranged around a series of colossal courtyards

ceremony, the ridge beam did not fit into the tenon, an inauspicious event liable to greatly embarrass and anger the emperor. Lei Fada, who was then over 50 years old, wearing full ceremonial garb ascended the frame and with a few blows of his hatchet coaxed the beam into place. The emperor was so impressed he made Fada head of the construction section of the board of works, a position hitherto occupied only by members of the elite civil service. When Jinyu, Fada's eldest son, succeeded to the official post, he became a grade-seven functionary, a high-status position within the administration. The 'Designers Lei' would retain control until the end of the Qing period, 200 years later. The Lei followed a very comprehensive set of procedures. First, drawings were made, followed by models of thick pulp with detachable roofs to show the interior. These would be presented to the emperor for approval.

A clear hierarchy was established distinguishing buildings by their size, type of roof and complexity of detail. The most important ceremonial halls were given double-eaved hip-and-gable roofs, supported by the overlaid tiers of interlocking arms and brackets called bracket sets. These allowed the columns of the Forbidden City to support a weight up to five times greater than would otherwise have been possible. The larger halls have bracket sets of extreme complexity, the smaller side rooms and galleries only employ single sets. The individual sizes of brackets shrank during the Ming and correspondingly the crossbeams running parallel to the eaves grew larger to act more like girders.

Multiple bracket sets increased the bending, sheer and compressive strength of the structure, as can be seen in the subsequent effects of earthquakes on the Forbidden City. The smaller corridors and terrace structures failed, but the Hall of Supreme Harmony (Tai He Dian), which supports over 2,000 tonnes of roof over nine bracket sets, stood firm. It was here that the ceremony of the emperor's enthronement took place, grand court audiences were conducted and the lunar new year was celebrated. The emperor would sit at the imperial throne from where he might survey the thousands of courtiers prostrating themselves before him, and reflect upon his role as son of heaven.

The theatricality and visual rhetoric of such events underpinned the remarkable achievement of the entire complex, most evident architecturally in the design of the corner watchtowers. These are built on a square cross plan. Their roofs are made up of three sets of eaves, which contain 72 special ridges. The first is formed by the intersection of two pitched roofs presenting four opposing gables. The two lower sets are each made up of four groups of interlocking hip-and-gable roofs. The resulting confection is entirely impractical militarily (unlike the Japanese castles it resembles) but rests upon colossal stone walls, the real fortification. The corner towers are merely pavilions built to be admired by those beyond the city walls.

BEDROOMS OF EELS

When the city of Kyoto was originally created, its grid plan produced narrow subdivisions of lots within each city block. Taxes levied on the amount of street frontage reinforced the tendency of Kyoto's merchant class to plan their town houses in very thin strips perpendicular to the main thoroughfare. This has resulted in a vernacular house type nicknamed 'Bedrooms of Eels' by Kyoto's citizenry.

More properly referred to as 'city houses' (*machiya*), those that remain here are testament to a complicated system of co-operation and interdependence between residents. They lived in neighbourhoods of orderly blocks of 40 family units, which were called *cho*. The *cho* were originally members of a particular craft guild and would be responsible for the maintenance of a particular local shrine. The *machiya*'s development was inhibited by edicts handed down by the shogunate of the Edo period (1603–1868), which forbade extravagant displays in merchants' houses and prohibited any construction over two storeys high. These laws represented a concerted effort on the part of the samurai class to suppress the social advancement of the merchant class. The houses consequently have sober façades, with screens and blinds featuring refined wooden and bamboo details.

Unfortunately the very close abutting of *machiya* made them prone to fire. Virtually no extant 'Bedrooms of Eels' date from before 1864, when a struggle to restore the emperor resulted in a fire being started, which then swept through the city.

The backstreets of Kyoto, along Sannen-zaka or around Shinbashi, are still full of traditional *machiya*, which serve as shops and tea-houses

CHAPTER TWO
NORTHERN EUROPE

Wooden buildings form the largest part of Scandinavia's architectural inheritance. Most are the product of the coniferous forests that stretch right across the region from Eastern Europe to the Norwegian coast. Even settlers in Iceland, where there are few trees, took wood with them to build houses.

The countries of Scandinavia have been politically integrated in various combinations at various times. Denmark and Norway, Sweden and Norway, and Sweden and Finland have at one point been united and, since the sixteenth century, all four have been staunchly Protestant. Until comparatively recently they were predominantly rural societies, with small populations spread over huge areas of land. Regional building styles tend to reflect variations in topography and climate, rather than following the borders of nation states.

Four separate techniques of building in wood have been used in Scandinavia at various times: stave construction; blockwork; framework construction with horizontal planks; and half-timbering. In Norway stave construction dominated in the Middle Ages before being overtaken by blockwork. In Sweden both techniques were extensively used in church construction during the Middle Ages, again to be superseded by blockwork alone. But in Finland blockwork has been used almost exclusively.

Some common techniques did develop right across Scandinavia, however, most noticeably in blockwork. The simplest way to interlock logs was to cut a notch on the top or bottom of the log. The advantage of notching the bottom is that it provides less opportunity for rainwater to collect and damage the weaker 'worked' part of the log. The simplest technique is a round notch, which occurs throughout Scandinavia.

There were also regional variations. In Norway there was considerable experimentation with the form of the notch – sometimes oblong, sometimes square. In Sweden the same type of joint was used but its positioning varied enormously.

To stack the logs, all Scandinavian builders used a technique

of 'tight wall construction', which entailed the cutting of a long groove in the bottom of the upper log in a stack in order to form a tighter bond with the log below it as it settled under the weight of the wall. For the most prestigious buildings, junctions were also worked in 'dovetail construction', eliminating the need for projecting ends. This was initially reserved only for churches; only in the nineteenth century would it spread to secular buildings. Later, when water-power saws were developed, it became possible to produce cheap planks to clad the building so as to conceal the technique of construction altogether.

ABOVE Fishermen's cottages, Nedre Fjeldsmug, Bergen, Norway, 19th century
LEFT The pulpit of Seglora church, Sweden, 1729, was placed against the south wall to maximize the light from the larger southern windows

RIGHT Detail of doorway, Tvieto Loft, from Hovin, Telemark, now at the Norsk Folkemuseum, Oslo, Norway

STAVE CHURCHES

The origins of Norway's stave churches are obscure. We have no conclusive evidence of where these complex forms came from. There must have been a tradition out of which they developed but it is not certain whether this was indigenous or imported or partly both. It is probable that earlier Christian and pagan temples used a similar wood-frame technique. Similar structures are also found abroad, most noticeably St Andrew's, Greenstead, in Essex, England, where timbers in the nave may date from as early as the ninth century.

However, the stave churches are strikingly unlike anything else in appearance. Their basic constructional system is very simple but its extrapolation has produced complex and elaborate architecture. It has been calculated that some churches consist of more than 2,000 separate elements, not including the roof shingles.

A stave church rests upon four groundsills – horizontal beams of timber resting upon a stone face. These sills are lapped at the corners, leaving a rectangle and eight projecting ends. The vertical posts, the staves, stand along the central rectangle. They are connected to each other by clamping beams, often with additional knee braces and St Andrew's crosses to make a sturdy frame. This frame supports the pitched roof of the nave.

Additional vertical posts were placed on the ends of the groundsills and the outer wall of the building ran between them. Then roofs were erected between the outer walls and the central frame. Often an arcade of similar but smaller design would be run around the whole structure.

Originally over a thousand stave churches were built in Norway during the Middle Ages. Now only 28 survive. The oldest is that of Urnes in Sogn, among the western fjords of Norway, which was built around 1130. Earlier churches have stood upon this site and the presence of even older graves laid on an east–west axis suggests the existence of Christian communities earlier still.

At Urnes the heavily decorated western portal and gable panels of a previous church have been retained in the north wall of the current structure. These display the final flowering of what has become known as the 'Urnes style' of carving. Initially the composition is perplexing. There seems to be no

division into primary and secondary elements; all are given equal weight. With time, however, it is possible to discern the general theme as a 'lion entangled by snakes'. The lion looks far more like a greyhound but is surely identified by its mane, carved beautifully in volutes. Its head appears in profile, with a long snout, fangs and ears.

The thicker 'snakes' are confusing as each of their long sinuous bodies ends in a hind leg. All curve in a figure of eight which culminates in them biting their neighbours or themselves. The whole design is rendered in very high relief, an effect given variety by the plane of the background, which curves away in the centre of each panel, increasing the degree of relief.

The rest of the church shows the influence of the Romanesque. The nave is supported by 18 closely spaced staves (although two are concealed), which make up a colonnade braced by semicircular arches. There are heavily moulded archivolts and cubical capitals with decorated shields furnished with carved figures and mythical animals. These forms are carved in a shallow relief with very sharp sides and detail outlined in deep grooves. The capitals are, of course, purely decorative, serving no structural purpose in a wooden building. In fact, as they have a larger section than the stave, they have had their corner pieces attached. Their shape suggests a fairly literal translation of the stone basilica form into wood.

Urnes once had an apse. The current rectangular extension is an addition of about 1600. Later that century, the Munthe family pew was added by cutting two staves and inserting a tie beam. The structure showed signs of fatigue and was then crassly cross-braced.

Borgund stave church was built shortly after Urnes, in 1150. It is a building of greater technical freedom and visual complexity, but is based on a similar core. If, on the one hand, the form

LEFT Detail of north portal, Urnes stave church. The 'Urnes-style' Norse sculpture shows a lion battling other creatures – this is the refined work of an artist of high calibre

ABOVE The north portal, Urnes, 11th century, shows the last flowering of Viking art before the influence of the international Romanesque style was felt

TOP Hopperstad stave church, c.1150. The nave has an early 14th-century baldachin to the left attached to the main structure and richly decorated

ABOVE Lomen stave church was built around 1175 and has been altered many times since. During the 18th century the sanctuary was widened and extended to the west

of the nave is a development of the Romanesque basilica, it may also be true that it refers back to older native models of wooden church design. The central structure consists of 14 staves out of which two, on the north–south axis, are truncated and braced by substantial beams. This creates a more balanced centralized plan with entrances from both the west and south.

Both a presbytery and a semicircular apse have been added, and the whole surrounded by an arcade. With medieval additions, this has led to a highly ornamental exterior. Six roofs ascend the spire in stages. Originally these were faced with moulded vertical planks. Later they were covered with shingles.

The highest of the main roofs are topped with gables with dragon's heads, a motif which was to become synonymous with the stave churches. The dragon and tendril patterns are features of the Romanesque and hence are of foreign origin. However, their employment is distinctively Norwegian; a clear example of how broader European influences have been tailored to Norwegian sensibilities. Certainly the shape of the dragon's heads have an exclusively Urnes-style shape. Inside, animal faces carved high up on the staves have a distinctively Norse pagan quality.

The nave of the church at Hopperstad more closely resembles that of Urnes, with a colonnade strengthened by a single clamping beam with a St Andrew's cross above it. The archivolts and capitals are also similar to those at Urnes but without the same degree of decoration. As superior clamping-beam techniques improved the rigidity of the frame it became apparent that fewer

staves needed to reach the ground. At Hopperstad 16 staves do so, at Urnes 14, at Borgund 12. Lomen stave church was built only 25 years later, in 1175, but here large arches had been introduced to carry the weight of the staves and, of the 14 employed in the central frame, only four reach the ground. The later stave churches are consequently much less compartmentalized.

In May 1349 a wool ship set sail from London bound for Norway and ran aground somewhere near Bergen. Fishermen boarded the vessel to find, to their cost, that the entire crew were

dead from the plague. The Black Death swept through Norway with cataclysmic consequences. Between half and two-thirds of the population died. It was to take 300 years for the population to return to its original size. By the time new churches were built again, the expertise of complicated stave construction seems to have been lost.

ABOVE Hopperstad stave church. The exterior was heavily renovated in the 1880s, taking Borgund as its model

OVERLEAF Borgund is the only stave church with a completely unaltered medieval exterior. The gable ends are adorned with dragon finials whose design suggests an international European influence

NORWAY
THE NORWEGIAN LOFT

It is not certain when building using horizontal logs, known in Norway as the 'lafte' technique, began. Evidence of it appears from around 1000, but only after the Black Death of 1349 did its use gain general currency.

Lafte, i.e. blockwork, construction places one log upon another. This is an extremely demanding process, as the joints have to be very accurate. It was also very slow – the building had to be left for a year after it was built to allow the walls to settle. This enabled the logs to form tighter joints both under their own weight and as the timbers contracted. Once the building had settled, openings for doors and windows could be cut. Grooves were then cut in the sides of the opening, allowing the building to continue to move without causing the inserted frames to crack.

Traditionally Norwegian farms had consisted of a group of lafte buildings. The first was a small dwelling house (*stova*), with a simple plan consisting of a principal room and one or two surrounding rooms. The fireplace was in the middle of the room and a hole in the roof let the smoke out. The second generic building type, the *lofte*, was first developed in the Middle Ages and served both as a storehouse and as a place to sleep in summer. This building type has been built in a variety of ways. A loft from Rauland, Søre, Uvdal in Numedal (after 1250), is entirely stave-built. But most early examples combine a lafte-construction ground floor with a stave-construction upper floor. The top layers of logs were used to cantilever the upper storey. This overhang, known as a 'jetty', was used extensively in both frame and log construction in many countries but was particularly easy to achieve in log building.

The Tvieto Loft from Hovin, Telemark, and Ose Loft, from Austad, Setesdal, show the classic loft shape. The former has a medieval core with an upper storey renewed around 1700.

The house's semicircular sills are tenoned to bulbous stumps which sit on groundsills of conical section, to keep the building as dry as possible, particularly during the winter snows, and allow rotting timbers to be easily identified. The jettied first floor not only protects the lower logs from the weather but also shelters the front door and staircase to the upper storey.

These buildings would have been arranged in groups belonging to the same extended family. Villages, popular in Denmark and Sweden, were less common in Norway, where the topography discouraged collective farming. Instead, additional houses and lofts would be built to accommodate sons as they married, creating smaller hamlets.

ABOVE Front façade of a stave-built loft from Rauland in Numedal, constructed after 1250
LEFT Detail of a loft from Rofshus, Telemark, now at the Norsk Folkemuseum, Oslo, 1754
BELOW The Ose Loft from Austad, Setesdal

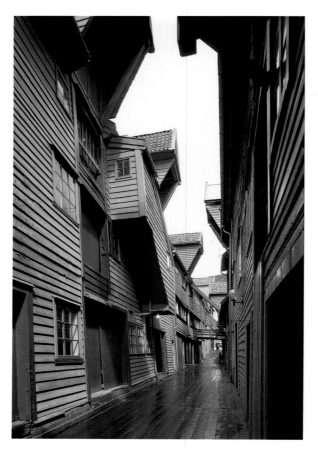

NORWAY
BRYGGEN AT BERGEN

In Norway towns were a comparatively late development. The three urban centres – Oslo, Trondheim and Bergen – only became properly established in the eleventh century. Little remains of early Oslo or Trondheim but Bergen still retains a large fragment of its medieval townscape.

Prior to Bergen's formal foundation by King Olaf Kyrre in 1070 the area of quayside on the eastern side of the bay had been colonized with warehouses. Here the settlement comprised long linear buildings with their gable ends overlooking the bay and accessed by narrow passageways paved with wooden boards. This area still retains the same basic form and is now known simply as 'Bryggen', meaning 'quay'.

Bryggen's remarkable survival owes much to its occupation for several hundred years by merchants from the Hanseatic League, a loose alliance of about 70 Westphalian and North German towns, the most important of which was Lübeck. They were first mentioned in 1358 and appear to have filled the vacuum in trade left by the Black Death. By the end of the fourteenth century the Hanse was the dominant force in the Baltic, and wielded economic and political influence from Novgorod in the east to London in the west. They established

privileged settlements for their merchants called 'counters'. In the late fourteenth century the Hanse established a counter in Bergen in order to monopolize the trade in Norwegian dried cod.

The all-male German trading post was allocated this part of Bryggen. Some of the buildings were owned by individual merchants, others by the whole community. The existing architecture was retained. Corridors ran the length of the buildings on the first and second floors. At the end of the passageways furthest from the quay were located single-storey 'firehouses' where food was prepared next to a two-storey *shødtstue* (or club) which included a public storehouse and tavern. Fire several times destroyed Bryggen, most recently in 1702, but due to its complicated system of community ownership, it was rebuilt each time as before.

ABOVE LEFT Between the houses of Bryggen, Bergen, run long streets at right angles to the quayside with overhanging lifting docks set below gable roofs
ABOVE RIGHT External staircases connect the buildings

LEFT & OPPOSITE Houses of Bryggen overlook the harbour in Bergen
OVERLEAF Employees were accommodated on the top floor of houses, grouped into rooms by rank

NAVE CHURCHES AND CRUCIFORM CHURCHES

Finland was almost ground flat during the Ice Age. When the ice sheets departed they left a range of glacial debris that dammed the rivers and created a huge network of lakes and channels. These split the country up but also provided varied possibilities for water travel.

Sharing its huge coniferous forests with Karelian Russia to the east, Finland maintained a tradition of blockwork architecture

in common with Eastern Europe. However, the religious and cultural influences of Western Europe and Scandinavia have dominated the style of this architectural tradition. Finland was ruled by Sweden for over 600 years and, like Sweden, has been staunchly Lutheran in faith since the sixteenth century.

Throughout the Middle Ages the Finns and Swedes built churches on a rectangular plan. These resembled masonry

FAR LEFT The west front of Pihlajavesi church, Central Lakeland, Finland, 1780. A 'pseudo-cruciform' design

TOP At Pihlajavesi logs oversail at the top of the wall to support the eaves

BOTTOM Supports for gutters at Pihlajavesi church are hewn from the springing point of branches. Gutters and a water downpipe are formed from hollowed-out logs

OVERLEAF Seglora church, 1729, now at Skansen, Stockholm, Sweden, is a 'nave church' design. Horizontal tie beams counteract the outward thrust of the roof on the outside walls

architecture with a long thin nave and a tower over the entranceway. The Seglora church, now at Skansen, Stockholm, of 1729 is a fine western Swedish example of this kind. When it was built each member of the congregation contributed a piece of wood to be used in its construction. The pulpit is placed to the south by the window; traditionally northern windows were kept small to minimize heat loss, letting in insufficient light for the pastor to read by. The sacristy behind the altar was only added in the nineteenth century when priests became self-conscious about donning their robes in front of the congregation.

Eventually the influence of the Italian Renaissance, which introduced the possibility of centralized square church designs, filtered through to Sweden and Finland. Perhaps the centralized form of St Catherine's, Stockholm, designed by Jean de la Vallée in 1656, was the conduit for these ideas. While the Renaissance would influence architects in eastern Sweden, the most advanced extant cruciform churches are in Finland. The speed at which the Renaissance influenced wooden architecture may be gauged by the fact that it was only in the eighteenth century that the Finns began to build with squared hewn timbers rather than round logs.

Change occurred in differing degrees, depending on how adventurous the parish and churchbuilders were. They were encouraged in their endeavours by religious practice and a growing population. The Protestant faith put greater emphasis than Catholicism upon collecting large congregations for Sunday services. In most parts of Scandinavia at that time, isolated rural communities would have found congregating in large numbers very difficult. However, the waterways of Lakeland Finland allowed large groups to meet by rowing themselves to church on flotillas of 'church boats' of up to 14 oars.

Assuming that large numbers of parishioners could congregate, the churchbuilders were still left with the logistical problem posed by Lutheran services which laid great emphasis upon the sermon: a major impetus to a more centralized church design was to accommodate as many people as possible within earshot of the preacher.

Many 'pseudo-cruciform' churches were built during the eighteenth century. These were essentially nave churches with the addition of large transepts. Keuruu (1758) and Pihlajavesi (1780) are churches of this type. Pihlajavesi was built for a congregation made up of ten holdings and four tenant farmers in a poor and isolated forest district of Ruovesi parish. It was built by Matti Åkerblom as an oblong, with a small south transept opening out of the nave and the north transept containing the sacristy. Keuruu was built under the direction of Antti Hakola, a self-taught builder, for a much larger and wealthier congregation. Here the transepts, while very much a secondary feature from the outside, form part of a large centralized interior space with ceiling heights close to that of the nave. They also contain galleries. To allow the congregation to hear, the pulpit has been placed at the junction of the nave and transepts. In the case of both churches the transepts provide additional

ABOVE The nave church of Seglora, 1729, now at Skansen, Stockholm, Sweden, shows a medieval form with the bell tower integrated into a rectangular plan
LEFT The blockwork walls of Petajavesi church, Central Lakeland, Finland, 1763–65, have interlocked joints

FAR LEFT The southern transept of the 'pseudo-cruciform' church of Keuruu, Central Lakeland, Finland, 1758

ABOVE Petajavesi church, 1763–65, has a separate belfry, built by the original architect's grandson in 1821

RIGHT The pulpit is supported by a carved sculpture of St Christopher and painted in 1779

FAR RIGHT The 'full-cruciform' design places equal weight on the nave and transepts

buttressing for the nave. However, both retain the Gothic tradition of an integrated bell tower over the entrance, however 'un-Gothic' its form.

In the fully cruciform churches of the latter part of the eighteenth century the transepts are expanded to the proportions of the nave. The parish church of Petajavesi, for example, has a ground plan in the shape of a Greek cross. It was designed and built in 1763–65 by Jaakko Klemetinpoika Leppänen, a native of Central Lakeland, in undisguised lock-jointed blockwork. Here the cross-braced barrel vaults of the nave and transepts intersect in a 'flat cupola'. The vaults have been decorated with groins painted with red ochre lines which conceal surface junctions. The carpenters are believed to have painted '1764', the year the ceiling was made, on the pendentives. Galleries in both transepts and above the entrance to the nave contained tenants and servants, while those who owned their own farms sat below, the men to the right, the women to the left of the nave.

The desire to centralize and enlarge the active part of the church led to the truncation of the corners of the Greek-cross plan. These 'truncated cruciform churches' replaced single right angles with two 135-degree angles. In addition, this meant that shorter logs could be used for the walls of the church, which necessitated less tree-felling in accordance with Swedish government edicts issued during the early eighteenth century.

In the church of Ruovesi (1777–78) there are no right angles but 24 angles of 135 degrees. Here, the now polygonal arms enclose an integrated central space 35m (115ft) across. Large windows light both ground-floor seating and galleries. A huge flat vault is held by two tie beams per arm. In total the church can accommodate 1,500 parishioners.

Building churches in Finland during this period required permission from the Superintendent of Public Architecture in

Stockholm, in accordance with royal decrees of 1759 and 1776. While Finnish church builders at Petajavesi did apply for and receive permission from Sweden, others ignored or partially ignored these instructions. Here Finland's peripheral status seems to have been an advantage as other Swedish church proposals of the same period were rejected and replaced with more conservative designs.

One common feature on both sides of the Gulf of Bothnia (between Sweden and Finland) was the proliferation of a 'Bothnian' type of freestanding belfry. These started to supersede the Gothic type at the end of the seventeenth century. Often they act as churchyard-gate belfries and commonly have a passage underneath. They tend to consist of three storeys,

diminishing in size as they rise, and are separated by curved roofs. The lower two are square in plan, the third octagonal.

The very late belfry at Petajavesi built by Jaakko Klemetinpoika Leppänen's grandson in 1821 illustrates the longevity of this style. Here the second storey contains a bell tower surrounded by an arcade of pilasters with shutters that can be opened to sound the bell. The classical details probably derive from the influence of the French Renaissance. Both the huge weight of the bells, and the structure of the tower itself, rest on a trestle of diagonal members, not unlike a child's swing.

There were many variations on this basic theme, not directly Bothnian in style, such as the earlier belfry at Kuru (1781), where octagonal upper storeys offset an onion-domed roof in a baroque gesture. In Finland these towers start with at least one log-built base storey. In Sweden the huge trestle legs were often exposed at ground level, protected only by shingles.

LEFT Detail of half-timbering
in house in Limburg, Germany
RIGHT Carved figures adorn
the timber frame of the Maison
d'Adam, Angers, France

CHAPTER THREE
WESTERN EUROPE

Western Europe has had such an extensive history of technological innovation that its early accomplishments in wood construction have been largely obscured by achievements in masonry architecture, and subsequently by innovations in steel, concrete and glass. Wooden architecture is remembered now only as a picturesque footnote to a history of Gothic cathedrals, classical houses and railway termini.

But wood was once the primary building material of Western Europe, whose forests were rich in hardwoods such as oak, ash, beech, elm and chestnut. These are more resistant than conifers to both fire and damp and their surfaces do not require protective treatment. A wide variety of trees were used but oak proved the most popular. Close-grained and very strong, oak is the least likely to warp or crack even when used green, and the survival of original oak timbers in St Andrew's church, Greenstead, Essex, for a thousand years testifies to its durability.

In Germany building in wood can be traced back as far as documentary sources permit. The Goths had their carpenters organized in an independent trade guild as long ago as AD 350. When Venantius Fortunatus, bishop of Poitiers, visited the cities of the Rhine in AD 560 he preferred wooden construction even to the masonry walls of Rome: 'Away with you, walls of square-hewn stone. Nobler far, I find, a masterly work, the carpentered building here.' Not only were peasant houses built in wood but so too were the palace of Attila and the fortresses of the Teuton kings.

In England wood remained the principal building material right up until the end of the seventeenth century. The majority of English towns, London included, consisted largely of wooden buildings. Manchester remained a predominantly wooden town until well into the eighteenth century.

Western Europe was, however, the first part of the world to seriously deplete its forest resources. Over 70 per cent of its original forests and woodlands have been lost and much of

this denudation happened very early. Half of France's forests disappeared between 1000 and 1300, the land instead being cultivated to cater for an expanding population. While over 1.6m hectares (4m acres) of trees covered England in 1500, reckless felling, according to the statistician Gregory King, reduced this to 1.2m hectares (3m acres) by 1688. The expansion of agriculture, shipbuilding and iron smelting were largely responsible. Forests were sufficiently threatened during this period to warrant legislation to control the number of trees that could be felled. Across Western Europe from the middle of the sixteenth century building in wood began to be overtaken by the use of stone and brick, except in places such as the Alps where timber resources continued to be plentiful.

Western European wooden architecture is often described as 'half-timbered'. The origins of this term are unclear. It is reputed to derive from the practice of literally cutting timbers in half before use. However, as most carpenters used instead the squared heartwood of a single log, it is rather misleading. In general it can be said to refer to a framed construction whose members are left visible on the outside of the building. The panels between the members are then infilled with a different material, such as brick or wattle and daub. Half-timbered structures are nevertheless as wholly wooden as the framed architecture of South-East Asia or North America (where timber infill panels and clapboards predominate respectively). Indeed, the clapboarding of North America is a direct import of Western European weatherboarding.

Wattle and daub consisted of small strips of wood woven to create a latticework mesh (wattle) and a mixture of clay, chopped straw and animal dung (daub). This was then covered with limewash. When properly applied, it was both waterproof and durable.

From the mid-sixteenth century wattle and daub was often replaced with bricks in a technique known as 'brick nogging'. This appeared to create a sturdier wall but actually had considerable disadvantages. The frame had to withstand the far greater weight of the bricks. Bricks were also more porous than properly rendered daub. Eleven-and-a-half-centimetre (4½in) bricks often projected slightly beyond the timbers to form little ledges on which rainwater might collect and rot the frame. But as brick production expanded, bricks became a viable economic alternative and their wide popularity was probably just a consequence of fashion.

One of the peculiarities of Western European half-timbering is the use of upper floors overhanging lower ones in a technique known as jettying. The exact reasons for this widespread technique are unknown. It probably started in towns where there was limited space at ground level, and from there spread to the countryside. In the absence of gutters and downpipes, jetties also assisted in keeping rainwater away from the walls. Perhaps, too, there were found to be advantages in counterpoising the internal load so as to reduce the effects of sagging inside. Also, their use requires timbers only a single storey in height.

ABOVE Timber bracing, timber yard, Geislingen, Germany
LEFT House in the cathedral close at Amiens, France
BELOW St Andrew's church, Greenstead, England

THE BARNS OF CRESSING TEMPLE

The Order of the Temple was founded in 1119 to protect pilgrims in the Holy Land. The name derived from the organization's headquarters in Jerusalem, which stood on the site of Solomon's Temple. By a papal bull in 1139, the Knights Templar became independent of any secular authority, answerable only to the pope and exempt from taxation. They used this dispensation not only to spearhead the military effort in the Middle East, but also to develop into one of the most powerful corporations in Christendom, with a large mercantile fleet, an international banking network and the ownership of over 7,000 estates across Western Europe.

In England, the Templars attracted the patronage of the crown, offering banking and safe-deposit facilities; indeed, the London Temple was the precursor of the Bank of England, holding the royal treasury from the end of the twelfth century. In return, the Templars received patronage; some of their most important estates were the gift of King Stephen and Queen Matilda, including that of Cressing in Essex. The great timber barns of Cressing Temple survive as monuments to the wealth and influence of the Knights Templar. The barns' survival indicates their vital importance to medieval agriculture and society. Here the entire corn crop, upon which the solvency of the estate depended, would be stored after harvest and threshed during the winter months.

Whether large or small, the medieval barn followed a standardized form for the storing and processing of grain. It was divided into three sections, two for storage and one for unloading hay and threshing. In England the threshing floor was traditionally placed across the central width of the oblong plan. Fully laden carts entered through a pair of double-height doors and, once emptied, left through smaller doors in the opposite wall. Hay was stored right up to the ceiling, direct from the cart. Then, during the winter months the corn was threshed with a hand flail on the floor of the barn. Finally, it was winnowed. The grain was tossed into the air with casting shovels, allowing the breeze passing between the sets of doors to carry away the lighter chaff while the heavier grain fell to the ground.

Both barns are aisled using arcade posts to carry the majority of the load of the rooftiles (some 55 tonnes) to the ground. Two side aisles with lean-to roofs complete the profile. The timbers of the Barley Barn have been dendrochronologically dated to the beginning of the thirteenth century, those of the Wheat Barn to its end. The Barley Barn used simple lap joints. Originally it was scissor-braced by very long braces running parallel to and against the rafters all the way from the ground to the apex of the roof. The Wheat Barn used a more sophisticated frame with fewer braces and rudimentary purlins held against the rafters with collars and cleats. These indicate the ongoing development of carpentry techniques during this period. However, the essential measurements of both buildings conform to multiplications or simple fractions of a medieval unit of measurement known variously as the rod, pole or perch (5.03m/16.5ft). Both buildings also share the use of strict geometric principles in their prefabrication and erection – the first agricultural buildings to do so. The Barley Barn displays an understanding of Euclidean geometry: it is the oldest known building to employ timber sills which would have required highly accurate carpentry to tenon the arcade posts into position. Moreover, both barns originally employed a

ABOVE & LEFT The Barley Barn (c.1150–1200) is 36m (118ft) long and 13.6m (45ft) wide. Five bays contain about 46sq m (500sq ft) each. In 1420 the lean-to aisle roofs, which originally almost met the floor, were truncated by side walls, making the barn shorter and narrower. The crown-post roof was added in the 16th century

very long passing-brace transverse timber which, in the case of the Barley Barn, ran the length of the roof and was lap-jointed in two places and, in the case of the Wheat Barn, was made up of two separate pieces. Both required a high degree of accuracy in the geometry of their construction.

The carpenters of Cressing Temple displayed a growing understanding of mathematical principles during the course of the thirteenth century. This was probably a consequence of contact with the Islamic world during the Crusades. Around 1120, Abelard of Bath had translated Euclid's *Elements* from Arabic into Latin, giving master craftsmen a proper comprehension of geometry for the first time. Techniques for building large wooden cathedral roofs had advanced rapidly during the last quarter of the twelfth century, coinciding with the introduction of the Gothic vault in masonry architecture. The Knights Templar were among the first Christians to use Arabic knowledge in the service of military engineering and were the first European soldiers to use the magnetic compass. As such they may have been able to add mathematical rigour to the practical expertise of their carpenters.

LEFT The Wheat Barn (c.1275) is 39m (130ft) long and 13.4m (39ft) wide. It was nogged with bricks at the end of the 16th century

ABOVE Detail of junction of arcade posts and plate in the Wheat Barn

Despite their many competencies, it is the Templars' spectacular fall from power that has ensured them historic fame. Acre, the final Crusader possession in the Middle East, fell in 1291 and removed the central justification for what was supposedly a charitable order of warrior-monks. Philip IV of France disliked and distrusted them, but also owed them money. He also dominated the pope, Clement V, and had had his predecessor, Boniface VIII, arrested. Accused of the usual array of medieval crimes – heresy, idolatry, devil worship, blasphemy and witchcraft – the Templars in France were arrested and tortured, and their confessions were used to force the pope to release a bill of suppression in 1312. He ordered that their properties be transferred to another Crusader order – the Knights Hospitaller. In 1314 the last grandmaster, Jacques de Molay, was burnt at the stake in Paris. Edward II of England was more lenient but after initially defending the Templars he plundered their estates and handed Cressing Temple over to the Knights Hospitaller.

THE WEALDEN HOUSE

The word 'Weald' derives from the Anglo-Saxon *wald* – a forest. It refers to that area of Kent, Surrey and Sussex that contained, at the time of *The Doomsday Book* (1086), the largest area of natural woodland in England. Here oak trees were once so common that they were known as 'the Sussex weed'.

During the next 250 years, 200,000 hectares (0.5m acres) of land were cleared and settled by pioneer farmers and small-holding artisans, turning this once backward district into one of the wealthiest in England. These were individuals who had made money through industry rather than feudal inheritance and who built compact manor houses but not 'great houses' like the landed aristocracy. Between the fourteenth and sixteenth centuries a consistent type of box-framed house emerged known as the 'Wealden type'. Its popularity reflected a design that satisfied the social pretensions of the yeomanry and did so on an economical scale.

A Wealden house consists of two twin-storey structures on either side of a double-height hall. The upper floors of these wings are jettied and, since the whole sits under a single steeply pitched roof, the central hall appears to recess, producing a distinctive indented façade. Curved braces support the wall-plate, which rises from the jettied wings, providing additional symmetrical emphasis and helping to distribute the weight of the ridgeline overhang.

Wealdens have a compact plan. Traditionally the front door opened onto a through corridor and from it the hall was accessed through a decorative screen. The medieval hall was the single space which established a landowner's social credentials, acting both as a formal dining room and as the estate or farm office. The head of the household occupied a central position on the high table, often lit by a double-height oriel window.

The double-storey wing behind the high table contained the private chambers, the parlour and the solar above. The parlour was used as a sitting room and private office, the solar as a bed

sitting room for the family. At Bayleaf, a Wealden house from Chiddingstone, Kent, the solar's special importance can be gauged by the high-quality crown-post and tie beam which supports the roof, and by the fact that it has a built-in privy overhanging the ground-floor wall. The opposite wing of the house contained the servants' accommodation, the pantry and buttery. Originally the occupants cooked on the fire in the open hall, but by the end of the Wealden period at the beginning of the sixteenth century, separate detached kitchens were added for baking and brewing – activities that were kept apart for reasons of safety.

ABOVE Headcorn Manor, Kent, 1516, seen from the churchyard. Many Wealdens show a high quality of detailed craftsmanship, with moulded fascias to the jetties and elaborate glazed oriel windows featuring moulded jambs, mullions and transoms

ABOVE LEFT The double-height window distinguishes the Great Hall accessed by two grand doorways oversailed by a flying bressummer supporting the eaves of the roof

There are many variations in the Wealden form and varying degrees of ornamentation in timber detail. The most elaborate Wealdens, such as Headcorn Manor in Kent (1516), have the distinctive Wealden façade repeated on the back and have jetties at either end.

The Wealden form was eventually replaced, not by grander but simpler houses, following a fashion set by the towns. At the end of the fifteenth century, while hundreds of Wealdens were still being built in the country, the importance of the theatrical show of the great hall declined in town life. Double-height open halls were replaced by houses consisting of two storeys throughout, with a continuous jetty rather than the indented Wealden façade. The hall simply became the principal ground-floor room, often with an open-trussed chamber above it, called an upper hall.

ABOVE Bayleaf Farmhouse, from Chiddingstone, now at the Weald and Downland Open-Air Museum

LEFT Crown post supporting the Bayleaf solar

LEFT The continuous jetty of Paycocke's House, Coggeshall, Essex

THE MEDIEVAL CHURCH

Throughout the Middle Ages the majority of churches in Western Europe were built in wood only in areas where stone was relatively scarce. The church of St Andrew's at Greenstead in Essex, however, suggests that this had not always been the case – its ninth-century wooden staves indicate that, in England at least, wood had been used instead of stone during the earlier Saxon period.

Even during the Gothic period of masonry architecture many stone-built churches were covered by open timber roofs. The greatest of these was the octagon added to Ely cathedral after the tower collapsed in 1325. This has a wooden lantern which rises 15m (50ft) above the roof and illustrates the technical virtuosity of the carpenters. However, few examples of exclusively wooden medieval churches still stand today. Other than a handful of parish churches, such as Melverley in Shropshire and Marton in Cheshire, it is mostly wooden belfries that have survived, such as the fourteenth-century example at Pembridge church in Herefordshire.

Stone churches also predominated in France. But in the Norman port town of Honfleur a remarkable wooden church remains. During the Hundred Years' War (1337–1453) between England and France Honfleur changed hands many times and in the course of one siege the church of St Catherine was destroyed. When the French victory at Castillon-la-Bataille in 1453 finally ended the conflict and drove the English out of France, it provided the people of Honfleur with an opportunity to rebuild. They had scarce natural resources but a strong shipbuilding tradition and the town commissioned local shipwrights to erect a new structure entirely in oak. The result is the largest wooden church in France. It has a very unusual plan, with two naves side by side, each of 12 bays. The first nave is thought to date from 1466, the second from 1497, when it was added to accommodate a burgeoning population recovering from the privations of the war. The tall oak posts support a central roof beam which runs the length of the church and from which tie beams spring on either side, while the structure is held together by hand-carved diagonal braces. Above are the roofs, whose gently sloping shape reveals their authors' hands in what look like the upturned keels of ships.

ABOVE LEFT The church of St James and St Paul, Marton, Cheshire, 14th century
LEFT & RIGHT St Catherine's church, Honfleur. North nave and south altar

ABOVE RIGHT Ely cathedral, Cambridgeshire, 1325. The octagon illustrates the engineering prowess of medieval English carpenters

TWO TUDOR INSTITUTIONS

Queen's is the only Cambridge college to possess a timber-framed building of any significance. Cambridgeshire had an extensive tradition of building in wood but the university had the wealth to replace wooden buildings with stone and, later on in the Elizabethan period, to embrace the fashion for brick.

The President's Lodge, built between 1537 and 1541, remains a fragment of Tudor architecture in wood. It consists of a two-storey building resting on the walls of the north cloister

jettying out about 0.6m (2ft) on either side, supported by a series of ornamental brackets, or consoles.

The top floor is split into a series of chambers but the first floor contains an uninterrupted gallery 3.6m (12ft) wide by 24.4m (80ft) long. This is lit on both sides by one large and two small windows, but these are not opposite each other. This was a common arrangement employed in the design of galleries in the sixteenth century. In a publication of 1561, the influential

French architect Philibert de L'Orme articulated the reason for its popularity: 'It will be better and have a handsomer effect, if the windows of the two sides of a room be not set opposite to each other; for, if they be so, there will always be shadows and obscurities produced between the said windows so as to make the rooms gloomy.'

The walls of the gallery have Elizabethan panelling ornamented with fluted and carved pilasters with lion's-head masks looking down from the cornices above them. On the façade overlooking the courtyard columns of wood support the large oriel windows. The outer walls seem curiously naked; they were originally covered with a lime plaster and animal-hair render common in Cambridgeshire. Now exposed, the timbers reveal the nail marks made when wooden laths were secured to the façade to provide grip for the render.

England experienced greater stability and prosperity under the Tudors as the country recovered from the ravages of the Wars of the Roses. But with Henry VIII's schism from Rome, and his dissolution of the monasteries in the 1530s, and then the religious guilds in the 1540s, greater pressure was placed on individuals to provide philanthropic donations for schools and hospitals.

ABOVE LEFT President's Lodge, Queen's College, Cambridge, 1537–41, seen from Cloister Court
ABOVE The group of medieval houses which make up Lord Leycester's Hospital, Warwick

Originally the guilds of St George the Martyr and the Holy Trinity occupied a group of buildings just within the Westgate of the city of Warwick. These functioned as both religious organizations and trade bodies which controlled the conditions of trade, maintained professional standards and oversaw apprenticeships throughout the city. When they were dispersed in 1546 their properties fell into the hands of the Corporation of Warwick. In 1571 Robert Dudley, earl of Leicester, acquired them and founded a hospital for ex-servicemen and their wives. It has survived intact to this day.

Lord Leycester's Hospital inherited the fifteenth-century guild buildings beside the Westgate and later took over two sixteenth-century buildings further down the terrace. This group overlooks the high street from their terrace and contains a variety of timber detailing. There are jetties on thin, forward-curving concave brackets with a moulded bressummer and closely placed studs.

Within the archway lies a courtyard containing a wooden gallery of two levels supported by four centred arches. The staircase, with its Elizabethan handrail, leads up to what was the Guildhall itself, originally the council chamber of the master and principal brethren of one of the guilds. It has an arch-braced roof, carved pendants and purlins decorated with carved foliage.

LEFT The original Guildhall of one of the constituent guilds was incorporated into the new Lord Leycester's Hospital in 1571

ABOVE The President's Gallery runs the length of the President's Lodge in Queen's College, Cambridge

OVERLEAF Four centred arches support a 15th-century double-height gallery in Lord Leycester's Hospital

THE MEDIEVAL TOWN HOUSE

The jettying of one storey over another was a very common feature in the urban centres of medieval Europe. The scarcity of space within a walled town encouraged both multi-storey development and jettying. In fact, jettying was so popular it warranted regulation. In 1410 the Council of Frankfurt restricted the first floor to having a jetty of one 'ell' (roughly a yard), and the next floor to a mere three-quarters of that. In Strasbourg, acceptable measurements were carved onto a stone tablet at the cathedral.

There were disadvantages to this system. The majority of timber frames used members only a storey in height. Without jettying the vertical columns could be placed freely across the façade to allow the placement of convenient windows within, as in the Old Town Hall at Bamberg. It was also difficult to create a jettied corner. This problem was overcome by different means in different countries. German carpenters adopted a form of multiple bracket that used three projecting beams to support the corner and both sides. In England 'natural' supports were often employed which were literally hewn from the relevant part of the tree.

The Maison d'Adam, in Angers in the Loire valley, was built at the end of the fifteenth century and offers a more metaphorical solution. A huge timber support for a jettying corner bay is adorned with a sculpted tree. In France it was fashionable to decorate the frame heavily and leave the infill panels relatively plain. Here a simple diamond lattice of thin timber strips adorns the panels while the frame is awash with a series of sculptures of contemporary life. Small figures cling to the upper levels of the façade. A dragon looks under the jetty to discover St George with his sword drawn. Two lovers embrace above the entranceway. Each gable is decorated by a spectacular curved flying bressummer, a detached arch which springs from the base of the roof pitch to support an additional frame under the eaves of the roof.

ABOVE LEFT Maison d'Adam, Angers, 15th century. St George lurks in wait under a jetty for his dragon
ABOVE RIGHT A disconsolate woman clings to a hewn upright
FAR RIGHT The full fantastical late 15th-century façade

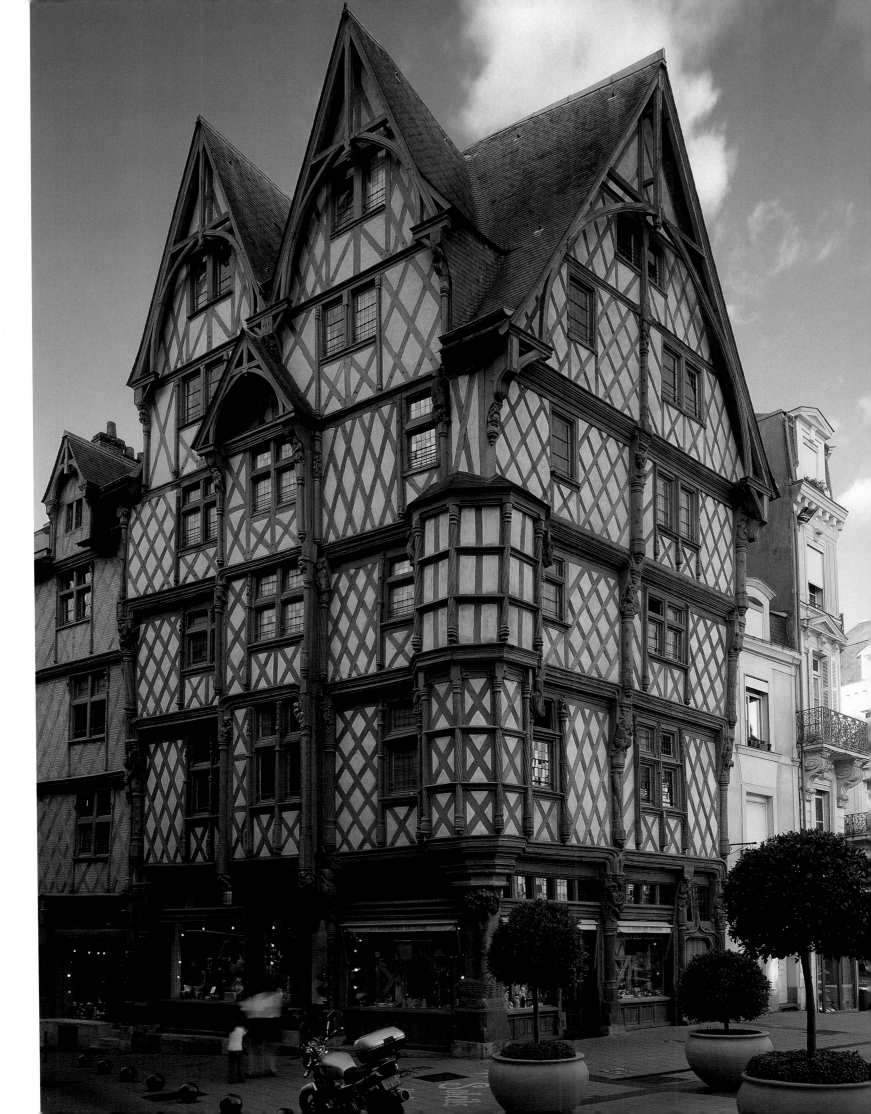

Jettying in Germany was altogether more muscular in character. The defining feature of the Alemannic style of half-timbering in southern Germany was the large gap between the posts enclosing wide panels in which small windows sit like eyes in the surface. The diagonal cross-bracing combined with the posts to form anthropomorphic figures variously described as the 'Swabian Wife' (*Schwäbische Weible*) or the 'Wild Man' (*Wilder Mann*). The projecting floor beams, which support the layers of jettied floors, were left as simple rectangles and set close enough to resemble a line of outsized dentils.

Built in 1589 by Martin Braun, a cheese merchant, the Maison Kammerzell, Strasbourg, illustrates the potential for compositional fluidity with timber-framed façades. The windows actually form a continuous linear strip, which wraps around the entire length of the two major façades of the building, flooding the three main floors with light. This design anticipates the slit windows of early International Style houses in France in the twentieth century and would have been impossible in masonry architecture. It was a consequence of the use of the 'spar roof', which gradually replaced the use of rafter roofs during the Middle Ages. Rather than using rafters that overhang the

ABOVE Schwäbisch Hall, Baden-Württemberg
LEFT & FAR LEFT The Maison Kammerzell, next to the cathedral, Strasbourg, Alsace. It shows both French and German influence

ABOVE RIGHT Town hall,
Esslingen, Baden-Württemberg
FAR RIGHT Timber yard, Geislingen,
Baden-Württemberg
ABOVE LEFT & OVERLEAF
Marketplace and streetscape,
Miltenberg-am-Main, Bavaria

supporting walls to form roof eaves, the spar roof used a horizontal tie beam fixed to the roof members to make a solid triangular truss. Because the rafters no longer oversailed the walls, smaller pieces, 'sprockets', were used to create separate overhangs. Here their use is visible in the abrupt change of angle of the eaves. The great advantage of the triangular truss roof was that it placed no outward pressure on the walls below, so the walls could afford to be much thinner.

Yet these thin façades are given great visual solidity by the profusion of timber decoration. Substantial corner posts articulate the junction of the separate planes of the façades and frame human figures – the centrepieces of the display. These represent Faith standing on an eagle, Hope on a griffon and Mercy on a pelican. On either side alternating window mullions and frames form a visual rhythm, embellished with carved human figures, animals and shell motifs.

BLACK AND WHITE

The rise of the Tudor monarchs after the Wars of the Roses established a new political stability in England. At the same time the development of artillery rendered the construction of castles irrelevant and focused the attentions of the aristocracy instead upon the building of great country houses. This trend developed during the reign of Henry VIII when houses such as Hampton Court and Layer Marney exploited the colossal boom in brick production. The dissolution of the

monasteries in the 1530s released huge quantities of ecclesiastical land into private hands. Established members of the gentry in political favour embellished their existing estates. But there also arose a new breed of courtiers and royal officials who took the opportunity to extend their credentials as landed gentry.

On the Welsh borders these men built their houses not out of the fashionable brick but of traditional timber frames. Little Moreton Hall in Cheshire is one of the most famous of this

generation of Elizabethan houses for which the phrase 'Black and White' has been coined. This refers to the later eighteenth-century practice of painting timbers black and infill panels white to heighten their contrast.

The earliest extant part of Little Moreton Hall is the north side of the courtyard which was built in the middle of the fifteenth century by Richard de Moreton. His heir, William, built the west wing around 1480. As the Moretons prospered under the reign of Elizabeth I, William Moreton II and his son John extended and restructured the property. It is uncertain why successive generations chose to extend in timber rather than

rebuild in brick or stone, but clearly, with a similar budget, it was possible to build a more imposing edifice in timber than in the more costly masonry. And the outward appearance of the building seems to have been of particular importance. The Moretons' concern with their social status is demonstrated by the lawsuit they brought against a neighbouring family in 1513 about who deserved precedence in seating at church.

When William Moreton II rebuilt the east wing and extended it south he added two huge bay windows immodestly signed 'This window whire made by William Moreton'. These windows provided some extra space for the hall and parlour, but seem

LEFT Little Moreton Hall, Cheshire, is covered with a wealth of ornamantal timber framing. The irregularities of its shape result from the excessive weight of the long gallery added in the 1560s
TOP The George Inn, Norton-St-Phillip, Somerset. Black and white window detail
ABOVE Pitchford Hall, Shropshire, 1560–70

to have been added largely for show. On the first floor they only light a small chamber above the hall. The final act of spectacular ambition followed in the 1560s, when John Moreton enclosed the courtyard with a south wing crowned with a 20.7m (68ft) long gallery. Its immense weight has caused the south wing to lean, adding to Little Moreton Hall's eccentrically picturesque shape. The aim, however, was surely a somewhat humourless grandiosity.

One of the implications of building large houses in wooden frames is that they are erected in structural modules. It is far easier to extend them vertically rather than on the ground, as Little Moreton Hall demonstrates. At Pitchford Hall in Shropshire

the rising fortunes of the Ottley family of wool merchants were expressed by the addition of wooden frames as wings to the existing building. The plan developed from a late-medieval oblong into an L shape and was then fully extended into its current E shape. Here the arrangement of a central porch placed between two flanking wings demonstrates the new concern with architectural symmetry.

A further, universal method of giving a structure social pretensions was to develop its cross-bracing into a decorative feature. The Feathers Inn at Ludlow (1603) features every conceivable kind of motif. There are lozenge patterns on the first floor, cusped concave lozenges on the second and a balcony running along the first with flat openwork balustrades. Three bay windows and three gables complement the multiple jetties and the asymmetry feels deliberate rather than accidental.

The Old Town Hall at Leominster by John Abel (1633) is a modestly proportioned but hugely decorated building with many carved embellishments. Shields and animal figures adorn spandrels and caryatids support sills. Timber could never compete with masonry architecture for monumentality but the Elizabethan and Jacobean builders showed that it had subtler means to convey the wealth and success of an increasingly affluent country. As an inscription at Leominster reads: 'like columns do upprop the fabrick of a building, so noble gentri dos support the honor of a kingdom.'

THE HALLENHAUS

For centuries the predominant agricultural building in the northern German states of Lower Saxony, Westphalia, Schleswig-Holstein and Mecklenburg was the hall-house or *Hallenhaus*. This three-aisled structure, with central nave and two lean-tos, is more closely related to monastic barns than purely domestic houses. It is uncertain how this particular form arose. There is evidence of three-aisled barns since 1700 BC, and at one time they could be found right across the eastern Netherlands and northern Germany. Surviving examples date from the fifteenth century right up to the twentieth. While there are regional variations in size, shape and detailed construction, they remain remarkably consistent in form. They were built in a post-and-truss system where stability is provided by continuous beams running across the top of the parallel rows of posts. These support a framework, 8–10m (26–33ft) in width, providing a central space (the *Diele*) of 3.5–4.5m (11½–15ft) in height and anywhere between 6 and 30m (20–100ft) long. The advantage of this system, which possibly accounts for its longevity, is that the outer walls support only lean-to roofs, not the main structure, and hence could be easily replaced. Often *Hallenhäuser* are found with earlier structures behind later walls. The hefty size and close-spacing of timber members on *Hallenhäuser* is a reflection of their near-universal use of brick nogging for the infill material.

Much like the monastic barn in England, the central *Diele* was accessed through a doorway large enough to allow a wagon to enter. The corn was then loaded into the space above the loft, and during the winter months the floor of the *Diele* would be used for threshing. Unlike English barns, however, the *Hallenhaus* was also the stable and farmhouse. Cattle and horses were penned into the side aisles while the far end of the *Diele* housed the kitchen and dwelling area with a central open hearth. This relationship was not entirely born out of necessity as the *Hallenhaus* tended to have a range of outbuildings as well. Instead there is an explanation for the obvious inconvenience of storing every sheaf of corn in the rafters which illustrates the social patterns of the people for whom hall-houses were first built. During the later Middle Ages, when the *Hallenhaus* form became set, the timing of the harvest would have been decided by the village as a whole, rather than the individual farmer. Harvest time was therefore fixed regardless of the weather. Invariably the corn would have to be stored damp, but by placing it in the roof space the farmer allowed smoke from the domestic fire to dry it and prevent it from rotting.

ABOVE LEFT Hof Meyer zu Bergfeld, 18th century
ABOVE RIGHT Hof Quatmann, 18th century
FAR LEFT & BELOW The Wehlberg, from Quarkenbruck, now at Cloppenberg, 1750. Heavy baroque brackets support the Wehlberg's jetties

HOLLAND

WOOD IN WATERLAND

During the Middle Ages great swathes of the Meuse, Rhine and Scheldt river deltas were forested. The name Holland itself derives from the word *Holtland*, 'woodland'. The region's trees were used to build dykes when a large part of the country was reclaimed from the sea in the thirteenth century.

Holland's windmills date back to the same period. They were used to drain the land by bringing up water with scoop wheels or wooden Archimedes' screws as well as fulfilling a number of industrial functions from grinding corn to mixing paint. Until recently, they were made entirely of wood.

In the Zaanstreek region north of Amsterdam wind-powered sawmills brought considerable wealth to the region during the country's golden age in the seventeenth century. Some of the wood came from local sources but most of it was imported from the Flemish Hanse to feed the expanding ship industry. The first wind-powered sawmill was built in 1592 and during the seventeenth century another 200 were built. By the end of the eighteenth century there were over

ABOVE A house in Broek-in-Waterland
LEFT Houses in Marken are raised on stilts to combat perennial flooding
FAR LEFT Detached houses overlooking the sea at Marken

1,000 working in the Zaanstreek. Today only seven remain.

Wood was used to build houses on the soft earth of northern Holland where the subsoil would not support masonry architecture, and outside the main cities where fire regulations against wood were relaxed. This vernacular tradition has survived with regional variations.

Houses in well-to-do Broek-in-Waterland have restrained Dutch gables in an elegant range of colours aping the forms of masonry architecture. The houses of the Zaanstreek show a rich decoration highlighted in white on houses painted primarily green. Generally they are single-storeyed structures, but with notable exceptions such as the house on the Kalverringdijk at Zaanse Schans, which has a platform frame. In this technique each storey is constructed separately and placed on the one below. So when the ground floor was finished it acted as the working platform for construction of the first floor.

On the island of Marken, tiny fishermen's cottages were grouped together on stilts on the highest points of land to combat flooding. They were painted black with tar to defend the timber against the salty air.

ABOVE & OVERLEAF Houses on the Kalverringdijk at Zaanse Schans show wooden decorative gables. The houses on the Zaanse Schans are typically painted green

TOP LEFT From left to right: oil mill De Os (The Ox), 1663; paint mill De Kat (The Cat), 1696; sawmill De Gekroonde Poelenburg (The Crown of Podenburg)

BOTTOM LEFT Canals have now been created in Marken to control the flow of water

THE ALPINE FARM

ABOVE Gosteli House from Ostermundigen, 1797
RIGHT The Gyger House from Adelboden, 1698
BELOW 'House from Brienz', Bernese Oberland, 1778

In the Alps the extreme climate imposed the need for self-sufficiency and the use of local resources. Fortunately, the Alpine conifer forests of spruce, fir, pine and larch contained plentiful building materials and a long tradition of log construction resulted. A timber member in a house in the Swiss canton of Schwyz was dated by dendrochronology to the year 1287.

The term 'chalet' originally referred to a type of simple blockwork hut in the foothills of Vaud canton, Switzerland. But since the nineteenth century it has been used to describe any Alpine-looking blockwork building. Many of our impressions of the classic chalet derive from buildings in Switzerland's Bernese Oberland. These have the classically low-pitched roofs covered with shingles or sheets of slate and weighed down with split timber and large stones to stop them blowing away. They also have ornamental and decorative touches such as wood-carving or wall paintings on their façades. Most of these houses sat on stone bases, usually containing a cellar.

The Gyger House (1698) from Adelboden, and now at Ballenberg, Switzerland, suggests that this external display was not always purely decorative. An inscription across the façade reads: 'Thomas Gyger built this house when he was 77 years old and his wife 71, so it came upon the world.' Gyger must have sensed the proximity of his own death as the first inscription is followed with ones entreating God's protection and verses from the psalms expressing contemplation of the Almighty. As a rather more superstitious precaution, the owners also attached branches to the edges of the roof to ward off evil spirits.

The high quality of the wood carving in the chalets of the Bernese Oberland is evident from the so-called 'House from Brienz' (1778). Here the façade is replete with decorative features, with protruding tie beams supported at regular intervals by small inset brackets.

Often one façade was clad with a covering wall (*Mantelmauer*) to give the house greater visual impact. A particularly good example is the Gosteli House from Ostermundigen, built by Benedicht Gosteli in August 1797. Its tiled roof terminates in a quarter-hip whose broad gable end emphasizes its impressive size. Painted imitation windows embellished by paintings of birds and cornucopias give the impression that this two-storey building has three floors. The balcony posts are marbled and the Gosteli coat of arms painted on the loft wall. Gosteli did not enjoy this display for long, as French soldiers shot him dead in front of the house in March 1798.

LEFT Church of the Holy
Archangels, Surdesti,
Maramures, Romania, 1766
RIGHT The octagonal tower of
the Church of the Assumption,
Kondopoga, Russia, 1774

CHAPTER FOUR

EASTERN EUROPE

The softwood forests of Eastern Europe are part of that ring of boreal forestry that encircles the planet around the North Pole. Further south, and at lower altitudes, grow a great variety of deciduous trees. Due to these abundant resources this region forms the centre of an enormous tradition of building in 'log construction' (blockwork). This stretches throughout Scandinavia to the North Sea in the west, as far as Asia in the east and as far south as the Black Sea and Yugoslavia.

Archaeological evidence of blockwork from 747 BC has been found in pre-Slavic Iron Age settlements at Lake Biskupin, near Poznan in Poland. The extensive archaeological discoveries of the medieval city of Novgorod in Russia reveal a remarkable wooden city paved with a decking of split logs laid flat surface upwards for sledge traffic. Remarkably, 98 per cent of its buildings were made in blockwork from untrimmed pine logs. The dominance of this technique was so complete that as late as the seventeenth century foreigners like Adam Olearius, who

travelled down the Volga in 1636, found wooden cities such as Tsaritsyn (later Stalingrad/Volgograd) completely built of blockwork. To this day hundreds of entirely wooden villages remain in the mountains of Romania, Ukraine and Slovakia.

The same procedure of harvesting timber was common across Eastern Europe. This involved chopping down the trees in the spring (before the sap rose) and then leaving them until the following winter. Construction would then begin the following spring, a full year after the trees were felled.

The choice of wood depended upon the topography and location. To the far north and in the mountains, only pine and fir were readily available. Elsewhere hardwoods were also commonly used and oak, which was recognized worldwide for its durability, was often employed for the massive basement framework members, while a softer wood might be used on top.

In the north of Russia whole round logs were used untrimmed – except for the removal of bark. Further south, in Slovakia,

Romania and Ukraine they were flattened off into a square section. The timbers were worked with both axes and adzes, notched at the ends and then laid on top of each other to form the walls. Where they were interrupted by doors and windows, the logs would be cut and their edges pared down to fit into the grooved uprights of window and door frames. The difficulty of jointing the logs at the corners so that they would hold together led to the development of more complex types of locking design. During the eighteenth century a very secure type of dovetail (called a 'German Joint') was invented which was so successful that it was adopted from Croatia to Ukraine.

Of all the wooden architecture of Eastern Europe, the style which developed in the greatest isolation was that of northern Russia. Here the colossal forest, the largest in the world, meant that the wooden tradition remained dominant well into the twentieth century. The distinctively Russian vocabulary of pyramidal roofs and onion domes derives entirely from the practice of wooden construction. What is most extraordinary is that all of this was achieved by the Russians' remarkable proficiency with the axe, which they used to fell trees, strip off bark, split logs to create boards and even fashion detailed decoration. Saws were not used as they would have opened up the grain, exposing it to the brutal climate; by contrast, the correct stroke of the axe actively closed the grain.

On the other hand, the influence of masonry architecture can be seen in the wood architecture of northern Romania, which is a peculiar and very late reworking of the International Gothic Style.

ABOVE Desesti church, Maramures, Romania, 1770. Wall painting in narthex
LEFT Oshevnevo House, from Oshevnevo, now at Kizhi Island, Russia, 19th century. Kitchen
FAR LEFT The Church of the Nativity of the Virgin, from Peredki, now at Novgorod, Russia, 1539

RUSSIA

THE RUSSIAN FARMHOUSE

The basic unit of construction in Russian architecture is the block-work square of four logs laid end to end: the *srub*. All Russian wooden architecture is an extrapolation of that procedure. The structures that most clearly express their constituent *sruby* are the generic farmhouses (or *izba*). These were sometimes erected by a local carpenter but were often the work of the farmer himself. They are generally found to have inherently satisfying proportions and are adorned with carved and painted decoration.

The typical farmhouse has two storeys and an outside staircase. The upper storey is residential, the ground floor housing the farm offices and many of the functions of the farm – stables, cattle sheds, haylofts etc. This arrangement, along with the external staircase, ensured that the farm could operate even when deep snow was banked against the building.

Farmhouses were generally quite small but could occasionally be of a substantial size. The farmhouse from Oshevnevo, now on Kizhi Island, is of a very large *koshel* ('basket') type. Its oblong plan accommodates all the functions of the farm in a single framework organized into two distinct sections. The residential quarters sit under a short steep roof, the active farm under a long gentle one.

The ground floor of the farm contained cattle sheds, stables and storerooms which allowed the farmers to work protected from the winter weather. Above was a storeroom for hay and agricultural equipment accessed by a long sloping ramp from outside, strong

enough to take a horse and cart. The upper part of the structure was supported by massive pillars which could be replaced individually without disassembling the whole building, even in the middle of winter.

The roof is entirely log-built. The log gables are cross-braced by rough untrimmed timbers called *slegi* which form the main purlins. On top of these, fir logs (*kuritsi*) serve as rafters. These have been specially felled to make use of the root sticking out at the lower end as a hook, in which the gutter beam is placed. The gutter beam in turn receives the lower ends of the roof's decking. Along the ridgeline runs a hollowed-out log called a *shelom*, or 'helmet'. This is fixed down by wooden dowels that run along the profile of the roof known as *soroki*, literally 'magpies'.

TOP & ABOVE LEFT Oshevnevo House, from Oshevnevo (named after the Oshevnev family), now at Kizhi Island, 19th century

LEFT Yelizarov House, from Medvezhegorsky, now at Kizhi Island, 19th century. Dining room RIGHT Ekimova's House, Rishevo, now at Novgorod, 1882. 'Baroque' details of first-floor window

THE ORTHODOX CHURCH

Christianity was only established in the hinterland of Russia at the beginning of the eleventh century, and the first churches must have closely resembled farm buildings. Simple country chapels continued to take this form, often only distinguished by a small onion dome. As members of the Orthodox faith Russian churches use the three-room plan which is thought to be of Byzantine origin. This was accommodated in three *sruby*, of which the easternmost housed the altar, the central one the nave and the final room, the 'narthex' in Orthodox terminology, was called the *trapeznaya*. Its name was derived from the Greek word *trapeza*, literally 'table' (hitherto used to describe the monastic refectory), and it functioned as everything from a place where the congregation could socialize before and after the ceremony to a court of law. The overspill of such assemblies could also use the covered porch and external staircases (*kryltso*), which became popular features of church design.

The pyramidal church form, so characteristic of Russia, is of uncertain origin. Fortifications predating the coming of Christianity already used an octagonal method of construction. Simply by arranging the logs in a polygonal shape the blockwork technique was used to create a chamber greater in length and width than the tallest conifer. The resulting shape, surmounted by a tall pyramidal roof, satisfied what appeared to be a perennial Russian fascination with height in church architecture. A small dome generally crowned the apex of the roof. This wooden form clearly went on to influence masonry architecture in Russia, as can be seen in the profile of St Basil's in Moscow (1555) and most obviously in that of the Church of the Ascension in Kolomenskoye (1532).

A common variation upon this type is the 'octagon-upon-a-square', to be seen in the Church of the Dormition from Kuritsko, Novgorod (1595), where an enlarged narthex wraps around the central nave. A more complex development of this theme can be seen at the Church of the Nativity of the Virgin, from Peredki, which is now at Novgorod (1539). This is cruciform in plan and is surmounted by steeply pitched roofs from which individual domes ascend. Its vertical thrust is balanced by a

ABOVE Church of the Assumption, Nikulino, 1599. A simple country church consisting of three *sruby* and distinguished merely by an onion dome
FAR LEFT The Church of the Nativity of the Virgin, now at Novgorod. Detail of covered porch and external staircases (*kryltso*), on cantilevered brackets
LEFT Church of the Dormition, from Kuritsko, Novgorod, 1595

gallery, which wraps around three sides of the structure. This is ingeniously raised above the highest winter snowdrifts by logs that project out of the walls to form cantilevered brackets or 'consoles'. These exploit an inherent strength of tree trunks: their resistance to bending stresses.

During the seventeenth century this kind of 'pyramidal church' fell foul of the authorities. Ecclesiastical reforms of 1653 promulgated by Patriarch Nikon, leader of the Purist Movement, prohibited the pyramidal roof form, demanding instead the adoption of five domes, the symbol of true orthodoxy. This resulted in schism in the Russian Orthodox Church. The dissenters or 'Old Believers' (*raskolniki*) fled north, away from the Patriarch's seat of authority in Moscow, and continued to employ the pyramidal roof. In fact, the greatest of the pyramidal churches was built much later, in 1774, on the shore of Lake Onega at Kondopoga. Here the Church of the Assumption displays an octagon, which actually expands twice before being crowned by a pyramidal roof reaching 42m (132ft).

Because of the church's extreme proximity to the lake a pair of staircases were installed along the north and south walls (instead of the usual western position). The building's monumental silhouette, whose height contrasts with the huge flat landscape around it, seems to be relieved by only one decorative feature – an ornamental course of timber. In fact, this is also functional as its members act as gutters leading to waterspouts

placed in the bottom of the dips. The whole ensemble is deftly balanced. The eastern *sruby* housing the altar is short and highly modulated by the sculptural ogee-shaped roof known as a *bochka*. The western extension is long and low, hugging the ground and contrasting with both the delicate staircases and the vertiginous pyramidal roof. It remains a poignant symbol of the aesthetic principles of the 'Old Believers' who would ultimately be suppressed.

ABOVE Church of the Assumption, Kondopoga, 1774. Two substantial columns support the roof of the greatly enlarged *trapeznaya*

LEFT Bratsk Stockade, 1652, now at Kolomenskoye, near Moscow. Detail of log jetty
RIGHT & OVERLEAF Church of the Assumption, Kondopoga, 1774

CATHEDRAL OF THE TRANSFIGURATION

When Nestor, the master carpenter, completed the Cathedral of the Transfiguration, he is said to have thrown his axe into Lake Onega crying, 'The world has never before seen, and never again will see its like.' The cathedral is the sole survivor of the multi-domed cathedrals of Peter the Great, built in 1714 during the Northern War against Sweden (1700–21), which established Russia as a European power. It was built on Kizhi Island in the

middle of Lake Onega in Karelia, an area which had been in the front line against Scandinavian invaders and which had, at the time, a large population.

The practice of building multi-domed cathedrals has a long history. Most influential was the famous oak cathedral of St Sophia the Great, Novgorod, which was built in the second half of the tenth century. All that is left of it now are written accounts. Nestor

took these familiar elements and combined them into a highly
original whole.

The composition of the Cathedral of the Transfiguration is
audacious, yet coolly logical. The central core is an octahedron superimposed upon a Greek cross. At the top, two further
smaller octahedrons ascend in tiers, finally supporting the
largest of 22 onion domes. Below, the roofs of all four stepped
tiers are arranged in the traditional ogee shape of a *bochka*.
Unusually Nestor integrated each to support an onion dome.
The final, twenty-second dome sits above the apse, which

extrudes out to the east at a lower level. The five tiers of domes
are perfectly integrated into the pyramidal shape beloved of the
Russian north, the shape being intensified by the silver aspen
shingles which contrast with the dark pine logs. Its overwhelm-
ingly complex elements are orchestrated into a single gesture.
Nestor was right: nothing comparable has since been built.

The cathedral forms part of a clerical *pogost* – a fortified
group of buildings, including a cemetery, common in northern
Russia. The *pogost* also includes the Church of the Intercession
where services were held during the cold winter months. Its

interior, like that of all Russian churches, has shallow enclosed ceilings, to keep the congregation warm. Outside, the building serves as a horizontal foil to the great cathedral with a display of nine domes presented on a shallow pyramid. The octahedron fits neatly on to a rectangular church body. The raised staircase is deliberately placed towards the cathedral – a bold asymmetrical gesture contrasting with the symmetry of the church itself.

However complex the wooden architecture of Russia, it continues to have a primitive visual feel which belies its subtlety. Logs of the same size were carefully chosen to create a 'log module', giving even utilitarian buildings a sense of proportional correctness. At the same time it reminds us that, while beautifully constructed, they are still clearly piles of trees.

Russians also took form-making in log construction to its logical conclusion. While it is just as easy to create a shape in frame construction, the advantage offered by log construction was its ability to create curves. The onion dome, Russia's most iconic architectural symbol, was built in much the same manner as the wall that supported it. First, short lengths of logs were assembled in octagons. Then a slightly larger version of each octagon was placed on top of the one below until the largest

diameter required was reached. Smaller layers were then added again. The whole was further carved with the axe to achieve a greater degree of curvature and then covered with protective shingles. Bizarrely, all this complexity of form was achieved using the simplest of jointing techniques. A single joint created some of the most remarkable and complex forms in wooden architecture.

ABOVE Twice the height of St Basil's in Moscow, the Cathedral of the Transfiguration was built to be seen from great distances across the island and the lake

RIGHT The Church of the Intercession's nine domes act as a visual accompaniment to the cathedral without competing with it

TRANSYLVANIA

CHURCHES OF THE MARAMURES

The Maramures is one of the largest depressions in the Carpathian mountain range straddling the Ukrainian/Romanian border. It is remote territory and was once in the centre of a vast Central European range of forests. In the early Middle Ages the density of trees made it almost wholly impassable and even as recently as 1900 woodland covered 55 per cent of the land. There are still dense forests of deciduous trees, especially beech, oak and maple; above them (from about 1,400m/4,600ft) grow the conifers fir and spruce.

Long before their conversion to Christianity, the population of the Maramures had developed an intensive woodworking culture. And almost to this day nearly all dwellings, household equipment and other utilitarian items have continued to be fashioned in wood – including cups, spoons, containers for liquid and even farm machinery.

In the Romanian section of the Maramures, which forms part of the wider region of Transylvania, there are still towns and villages wholly constructed from wood, and some 800 remaining wooden churches. The most remarkable of these are among the greatest achievements of indigenous 'folk' architecture anywhere in the world.

While the area is very isolated it is also, paradoxically, at a cultural crossroads, and these mixed influences have penetrated into its narrow valleys and isolated ravines. Romanians are ethnically a Latin people and have traditionally strong cultural ties with the countries to the west, but, like the Moldavians, their neighbours to the east, the population is predominantly of the Eastern Orthodox faith. Historically Roman Catholics, whether Hungarian or Austrian, have wielded political power here. The unique tradition of wooden architecture in the Maramures draws on all these influences. The exteriors of the buildings are formally acceptable to the Catholic eye, but their low dark interiors reflect the sensibilities of the Orthodox Church.

The region's inaccessibility has also ensured a degree of autonomy, albeit within an anachronistic political structure. The late survival of the Gothic language of architecture reflects the fact that until the beginning of the nineteenth century the people of the Maramures were a peasant community whose lives and land were officially owned by a remote aristocracy. As long as this feudal society remained, so did the habits of the Middle Ages, including the continuing use of the International Gothic style. The Maramures continued to develop and perfect

ABOVE LEFT Church of the Presentation of the Virgin at the Temple, Barsana, 1720
FAR LEFT The belfry of the Church of the Holy Archangels, Surdesti, 1766

ABOVE RIGHT & BELOW Church of St Nicholas, Budesti Josani, 1643, and detail of carvings on the west portal

ABOVE Church of the Holy
Parasceve, Poienile Izel, 1604.
Detail of wall recessed at upper
level, an 18th-century addition

ABOVE Church of the Holy
Archangels, Surdesti. The west
front is decorated with a series
of semi-circular arches, whose
profile displays 'crockets'
similar to those of the medieval
Gothic arch

RIGHT Church of the Holy
Paraskeva, Desesti. Ventilation
openings project from the ridge-
lines of the apse and nave

its version of Gothic in wood in a series of churches of ever
greater daring and complexity right up until the end of the
eighteenth century.

In the Maramures the tradition of timber churches seems
to have developed naturally from the older tradition of timber
houses. These used blockwork (or *blockbau*) techniques to construct walls from logs. Logs were hewn on all four sides and then
fitted together by one of a number of kinds of flush jointing.

Similar ceremonies were performed in both house and
church, such as prayers for the soul of a dead relative and a
ceremony at the birth of a child where the newborn's head
was lifted to touch the central beam of the house. Both house
and church entrances were protected by similar large carved
crosses. Originally devoid of towers, what distinguished church
from house was the addition of a rectangular apse, such as in
the church at Poienile Izel, first built in 1604. This rectangular
extension was replaced by the truncated five-sided apse at a
later date.

The standard plan followed the practice of the rest of the Orthodox Church in Romania and included a narthex (or pronaos),
nave (or naos) and sanctuary (apse). In time decorated porches
were added, although they were not essential. Unusually, the
principal roof became divided into two separate sections at
different heights, the lower section being continuous with the
roof of the porch. The recessing of the upper wall of the nave
decreased the width of the barrel vault above the nave and at
the same time increased the width of the building's base. The
lower roof section protected the indentation of the wall as
well as freeing up space above for high-level windows. These
innovations occurred during the seventeenth century and can
be seen in large churches such as that at Budesti Josani with its
nave vault of almost 8m (26ft).

The earliest towers included in the original structure date from around 1600. Originally there was no need for a bell tower, as the *toacã* (resonating board) provided the call to worship. However, the tower was to take on great significance for the carpenters of the Maramures.

Tower design originally derived from medieval fortified masonry structures, as can be seen in the wooden overhanging gallery, which reinterprets the pattern from machicolated defensive structures. What was of fundamental importance in determining the heights reached by the towers was the practice of using a timber-framed roof structure above *blockbau* walls. Blockwork roofs required a tapering above a very wide base in a pyramidal or cupola form, as in Russian wooden architecture. In the Maramures carpenters instead chose to construct towers over the narthex which were made up of a framework of vertical members braced by diagonal beams from the height of the roofline.

During the seventeenth and eighteenth centuries taller and taller structures were developed as technical problems was mastered. In addition, the degree of decorative embellishment increased. Distinctly different styles of tower developed simultaneously around the Maramures by varying the proportions of the constituent shaft, spire and gallery. Often four small pinnacles were added to the corners of the central pinnacle.

The church at Surdesti, dating from 1766, in many ways represents the culmination of this tradition. The tower rises 54m (177ft), three times the length of the church. It is the tallest oak building in the world, and arguably the tallest of any building that uses timber jointing. The belfry sits high above roof level, a horizontal projecting course linking it visually to the steeply pitched roof below. The entire slender form is both heavily reminiscent of the International Gothic style and unmistakably Transylvanian.

LEFT & ABOVE Church of the Holy Archangels, Surdesti, 1766. The dark vaulted interior of the nave reflects Orthodox sensibilities

TURKEY

YALI ON THE BOSPHORUS

Originally the Turkic tribes were nomadic, roaming an area from Mongolia to the Eurasian steppes. They were shamanists who worshipped the spirits of nature and the weather. While most tribesmen lived in tents, the Uygurs are believed to have developed the Turkish house plan, incorporating into its design a mixture of shamanistic beliefs and Chinese Buddhist symbolism. They perceived the world as a square plateau floating in a celestial ocean. Thus, their buildings are said to have had a cruciform plan, corresponding to the four cardinal compass points of the universe. The Uygurs' successors, the Seljuks, converted the Turkish tribes to Islam, before they were themselves overtaken by the Ottomans, who in 1453 were to take control of Constantinople. Nearly all Ottoman domestic architecture was wooden. It was in the seventeenth century that the tradition of building yali, wooden houses and palaces, developed along the banks of the Bosphorus. However, the layout of these houses, which involved a central courtyard, with a *harem* (women's quarters) on one side and *selamik* (men's quarters) on the other, appears to have been inherited from previous centuries – an inheritance adapted to a hot, moist maritime environment.

The Italian traveller Pietro della Valle visited Istanbul in 1614 and described a half-timbered frame technique similar to that in Western Europe: 'They first build the timber frame as in the ships and cover it by boards from outside. The filling is of mud-brick or simple adobe.'

The builders used closely spaced studs and treated the internal wall with a form of wattle and daub where plaster was applied to laths nailed to the frame. A number of timbers were

ABOVE 'Ottoman Rose'-coloured yali, Ortaköy, European shore
FAR LEFT Crumbling façade of a yali, Bebek, European shore

LEFT Waterfront yali on the European shore

ABOVE Details of houses from Ortaköy and Bebek, European shore

used, including juniper, cedar, hornbeam and even poplar, but the most widely used was pine (*cam*). Hardwoods such as oak (*mese*) and chestnut (*kestane*) were used for wealthier properties. The markets of Istanbul sold standard timber elements such as beams, rafters and boards. Roofs were tiled and wooden outer walls painted a rich terracotta red, sometimes referred to as 'Ottoman Rose'. The houses were built over the Bosphorus on wooden piles with large bay windows, maximizing the benefits of breezes. A system of movable screens was also evolved so that the ventilation of rooms could be adapted to winter and summer conditions.

As early as the 1720s, the Turkish chronicler Kucuk Celebizade Asim Efendi noticed that a variety of new colours was being used for house painting, presumably a consequence of the influence of European tastes and fashions. The Ottomans were to regulate this trend so that the light pastel colours were reserved for Turks only, with the Armenian community being compelled to confine themselves to red, the Greeks to a leaden grey colour, while Jews, who were the descendants of the community expelled from Spain in 1492, had to paint their houses black.

The nineteenth century saw further European influence with the creation of an eclectic style of borrowed motifs. While some stylistic details were very definitely oriental, with screened

windows protecting the *harem* and Chinese gables, others were highly Westernized, including the introduction of a *piano nobile* storey. Often the woodwork is very decoratively carved, particularly the roof eaves. These were often cantilevered by finely detailed brackets and were decorated with geometric patterns, which, in the twentieth century, would show the influence of Art Nouveau. In 1839 the Englishwoman Julia Pardoe summarized the aesthetic: 'They are as fanciful, and almost as frail as fairy palaces.'

Turkey's transformation into a republic after World War I involved the repudiation of the culture of the Sultans. The traditional yali became damaged by association. Even up until the 1950s, huge numbers survived along the banks of the Bosphorus. But since then, the rapid urbanization of Istanbul and a lack of adequate planning controls have badly damaged one of the richest and oldest wooden traditions.

LEFT 19th-century yali blended Western and Eastern motifs. Cantilevered bay windows and weatherboarding are adorned with Byzantine domes, screened windows and Islamic patterns

RIGHT 19th-century yali at Yenikoy, European shore, with deep eaves. Screened windows refer back to earlier 'jalousie' screens used to protect the *harem* from outside view

LEFT The bell tower of
the Second Congregation
of Hingham church, Massa-
chusetts, 1742
RIGHT Green Street,
San Francisco

CHAPTER FIVE

AMERICA

When the first European settlers arrived in North America they found 45 per cent of this vast continent covered in forest. In New England, the first trees to be used as timber were the familiar hardwoods oak and chestnut. But there were also forests of white, red and jack pine as well as spruce. Over the course of colonization the pine forests of the Great Lakes were found to be a superb source of commercial timber, and here the logging industry developed rapidly. The trees were felled during the winter months when the ground was frozen, lashed together and moved on sleds along icy paths that had been sprinkled with water. When the spring came logs would then be released into the rivers and guided downstream.

The final sources of timber to be harvested were the huge trees of the West Coast, a band of softwood forests that ran down the coast 48–240km (30–150 miles) wide and over 1,600km (1,000 miles) long. In California the redwoods made excellent building timber, and in Oregon and Washington the

Douglas fir was used. Here, without the bitter winters, a 'skid-road' was invented to bring logs to the riverside. A path was cleared and felled trees laid at intervals, their trunks half-buried in the ground. These were dabbed with grease to allow the logs to slide over the top.

Timber remained an important part of the American economy for 300 years following colonization. The quality of these natural resources extended the tradition of building in wood long after it had become unpopular in Western Europe. At the end of the eighteenth century Thomas Jefferson complained: 'The unhappy prejudice prevails that houses of brick or stone are less wholesome than those of wood.' This was at a time when there were still four times as many people employed as carpenters than in all the other building trades put together. The taste for wood remained so marked that it seemed acceptable for a Texan plantation to house its slave quarters in high-quality local limestone while the Great House was crafted

from timber hauled all the way from the port of Galveston. During the nineteenth century the Industrial Revolution, far from replacing timber, positively encouraged its production. The balloon frame, invented in the 1830s, replaced complex wooden jointing with iron nails and ultimately enabled the swift manufacture of whole wooden cities.

From the establishment of New England, through Independence, the Californian Gold Rush and the development of a sophisticated American architectural tradition, wood has remained America's primary house-building material.

 Whipple House, Ipswich, Massachusetts, c1655

TOP RIGHT Hunter House, Newport, Rhode Island, 1748

RIGHT Laundry and machine shop, Hancock, Massachusetts, c.1790

THE FIRST COLONISTS

Of the earliest colonists that arrived in the 'Great Migration' of the 1630s and 1640s the vast majority came from the east and south-east of England. The settlers were predominantly of the artisan and middle classes and contained a high proportion of trained carpenters among their number. They brought with them a centuries-old tradition of timber-framing and techniques of construction that were to survive a full century longer in New England than back at home.

The vast majority of colonists before the English Civil War in the 1640s were moving to escape religious persecution rather than to seek their fortune. They founded small centrally planned agricultural communities around a central meeting house, close enough together for effective defence against the Indians. Once a village reached a certain size they would simply establish another one a few miles away. These settlements were carefully planned and, following the experience of timber shortages at home, they regulated the felling of trees despite the vast supplies available. As Dedham town records state in December 1667, indiscriminate felling was judged 'very prejudicial at present, but especially for the succeeding generations which it concern us to consider'.

Lime was not readily available in North America – a key ingredient both in mortar, and hence masonry construction, and in wattle and daub, which was used to infill frames in England. Instead the settlers used the less common 'weather-boarding' technique, where horizontal boards are overlapped and pegged onto the outside of the studs. This gave the ubiquitous New England 'clapboarding' technique.

The characteristic smaller East Anglian farmhouse of the early seventeenth century was a building of two ground-floor rooms, with chambers above, reached by a winding stair alongside the central chimney. Exactly the same layout can be seen today in the Fairbanks House at Dedham, the oldest surviving New England farmhouse.

Jonathon Fayerbanke had left Yorkshire in 1633 and moved first to Boston and then to Dedham when it was founded in September 1636. He was granted 12 acres of land and four of 'swampe'. The house he built sits on groundsills laid on low foundation walls. The timbers would have been felled and shaped with an axe and trimmed with an adze or sawn with a pit saw. Tenons were hand-sawn and mortises made with an auger and squared with a mallet and chisel. Without the luxury of an existing property to live in, timbers must have been used

LEFT Joseph Capon House, Topsfield, Massachusetts, 1683. This village parson's house was raised on 'Jun Ye 8, 1683', as it says on its oak frame

ABOVE Hoxie House, Cape Cod, Massachusetts, c1665, seen from the north. An example of the 'saltbox' profile

green, shortly after being felled. The hefty members of the house frame, once assembled, would have been raised into place under the direction of a carpenter in a carefully choreographed sequence, a practice that persisted in rural New England until the late nineteenth century.

Evidently Fayerbanke prospered, for he took an active role in town meetings and committees and received additional land grants dated 1637, 1642, 1644 and 1656. During the same period he made regular additions to his house. Firstly, a lean-to containing two rooms was added to the back. Then a new wing, virtually a separate house, was added to the east end, possibly for his eldest son, John, and his wife, who married in 1641. The west wing of 1654, although connected with the hall by a door and a step, is also a separate structure and is believed to have been used as chambers for hired men. These wings both have gambrel roofs, whose dual angles of incline follow a typical English design. Their independence of the original building is tacitly referred to by Fayerbanke in his will leaving 'all my houses' to his son John.

The original Fairbanks building with its lean-to addition was to become a particularly common form in Massachusetts in the seventeenth century. This asymmetrical profile invited comparison with traditional household saltboxes and has become known as the 'saltbox' type. A typical example of the freestanding saltbox survives on Cape Cod, the Hoxie House, dating from the mid-seventeenth century.

This house was built with a particular seventeenth-century 'plank' construction method. This used a frame with hewn sills, corner posts, plates and girts but without studs. Instead, sawn planks 30–45cm (12–18in) wide were nailed vertically to the plate above and the sill below. Then the clapboards, or in this case shingles, were nailed directly to the planks. The same system was used on the roof where solid planks were nailed to the simple hewn trusses with purlins (but without rafters), and then again sheathed with shingles. Inside, riven lath and plaster were applied directly to the planks, leaving a wall just a few inches thick, so that the windows protrude on the exterior.

While plank construction was to decline in popularity during the eighteenth century, the compact storey-and-a-half house, often in saltbox profile, was to become one of the ubiquitous house types in American architecture – the 'Cape Cod House'.

The first generation of houses were built swiftly, out of necessity, and tended to be enlarged as their residents became established. A significant proportion of two-room houses started life as one room. The Whipple House at Ipswich, Massachusetts, was doubled in size in 1670 by the founder's son, Captain John Whipple, who had made good use of a licence of 1662 'to still strong water… and retail not less than a quart at a time and none to be drunk in his house'. The expansion placed the chimney centrally in a façade which is actually still asymmetrical. Whipple also added jetties at either end of the house whose supports are hewn rather than framed. This is arguably the first evidence of an eye for fashion affecting the pragmatics of building construction in New England.

ABOVE LEFT Fairbanks House, Dedham, Massachusetts, c1637. View along the lean-to, the oldest example of this kind of appendage in New England, which housed the kitchen and the pantry

ABOVE RIGHT Detail of first-floor window in the earliest core of the building

FAR LEFT & OVERLEAF West wing with gambrel roof added in 1654; and view from the south

In Salem, Massachusetts, surviving buildings also display evidence of expansion. The John Turner House, whose picturesque appearance provided the model for Nathaniel Hawthorne's novel *The House of Seven Gables*, is a product of extensive remodelling. Turner was a successful mariner whose original house was of a two-room plan. Prosperity allowed him to add, around 1678, the large south wing and a two-storey porch in the angle between it and the old house. The new wing, which largely covers the old façade, was built on a larger and more elaborate scale, with higher studded rooms, double casement windows

LEFT Whipple House, Ipswich, Massachusetts, c.1655. A jetty was added to the east end in 1670 which was hewn rather than framed

ABOVE The John Corwin or 'Witch' House, Salem, Massachusetts. John Corwin acquired the house in an incomplete state in February 1675 from Captain Nathaniel Davenport of Boston

TOP John Turner House, Salem, Massachusetts, c.1668. At one time it had 14 rooms and eight gables

and jetties with carved pendants. He died in 1692, leaving his estate to his 21-year-old son, John Turner II, in the midst of the Salem witch trials. Inside the now defunct original chimney he built a secret staircase, presumably to hide one of his four sisters, were they to be accused.

John Corwin, of the John Corwin or 'Witch' House, served as a magistrate during the trials, and many of those suspected of practising witchcraft were brought to his house for pre-trial examination. The fine façade with entirely jettied second storey and drop pendants befitted his elevated status in the community.

FROM MEETING HOUSE TO CHURCH

The early villages of Massachusetts Bay were tight-knit puritan communities. One consequence of their non-conformist beliefs was the need for an entirely new congregational building. The meeting house is a building type that has no immediate predecessor in England, for English dissenters had gathered in any building that would receive them.

Puritan services abandoned the altar and placed great importance on the spoken word and hence the pulpit. Keeping the congregation as close to the pulpit as possible meant the rejection of the linear nave and the adoption of a square plan. Consequently meeting houses were to borrow aspects of the private house and reject wholesale the Gothic tradition of the Anglican religion.

The Old Ship at Hingham, Massachusetts, of 1681 is the oldest surviving meeting house built in the English colonies. It was built in a simple style, with a plain symmetrical five-bay

façade offset by a hipped roof and lantern. The £430 cost of construction was paid for directly by the 143 members of the congregation. The hall is wider than the nave of any English Gothic cathedral and is alleged to have been built by ships' carpenters who inverted the design of a ship's hull to provide a frame capable of spanning the 13.7m (45ft) room.

During the eighteenth century the puritans became less averse to the idea of the sanctity of a place of worship and the word 'church' appears more frequently. Gradually meeting houses were replaced by churches of the new classical designs which were sweeping across New England.

ABOVE & OVERLEAF The Old Ship Meeting House, Hingham, Massachusetts. The frame was raised on 26–28 July 1681 and opened on 8 January 1682

RIGHT Second Congregation of Hingham church, Hingham, Massachusetts, 1742

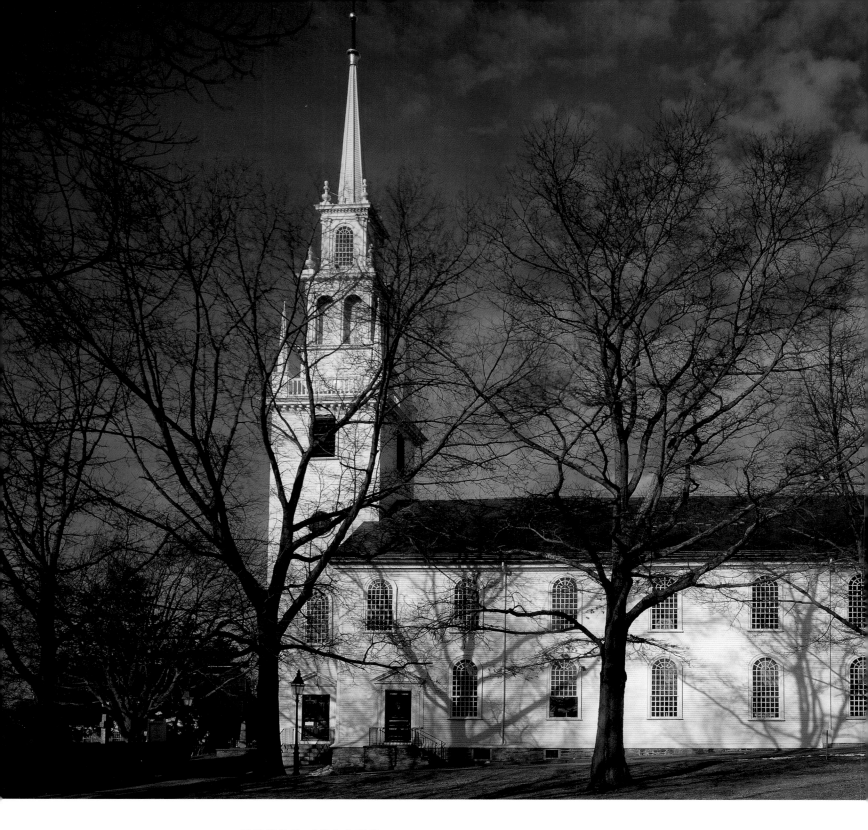

RHODE ISLAND

WREN, NEWPORT AND TRINITY CHURCH

When Dean Berkeley of Trinity College, Dublin, arrived at Newport in 1729 he found 'four sorts of Anabaptists besides Presbyterians, Quakers, Independents, and many of no profession at all... they are all agreed on one point, that the church of England is second best'.

In the 90 years that preceded Berkeley's visit, Newport had grown from a tiny hamlet to a town of nearly 3,000 people. Its

wealth was assured by the lucrative trade in molasses, rum and slaves. Unlike the other burgeoning cities of Boston and Philadelphia, Newport was built almost entirely of wood.

Three years before Berkeley's arrival an 'innkeeper and house builder', Richard Munday, had been entrusted with designing a new Trinity Church, the main Anglican church in the centre of the town. His design borrowed heavily from the recently

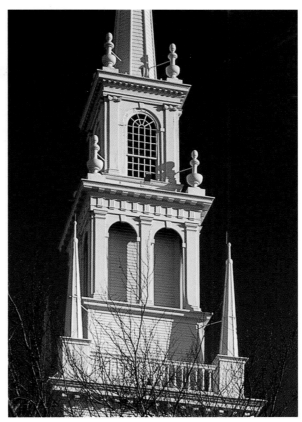

his own interpretation of the classical style. The naves of Christchurch, Boston, and Trinity Church, Newport, closely resemble the Wren churches St Stephen's, Holborn, and St Andrew's by the Wardrobe. Their spires are thought to derive from Wren's St Lawrence Jewry.

Munday transposed this Baroque masonry architecture into wood with panache, juxtaposing the heavy massive forms, such as the pediments, with details of great delicacy, such as the pilasters. His use of wood would prove advantageous when, in 1762, the growth of the parish necessitated a longer nave. The end of the church was simply sliced off and moved 9m (30ft) in order to accommodate two new bays. Now, with its semicircular apse at one end and 5.5m (18ft) square porch at the other, it reaches 38m (125ft) in length. The four-part spire rises from the roof of a tower, flanked by four corner spires set on bases supporting balustrades, the whole reaching a total height of 41m (135ft).

completed Christchurch in Boston — both suggest that the Society for the Propagation of the Gospel in Foreign Parts was in a position to offer the colonists assistance in the design of their new churches. Whatever the people of Newport's view of the Church of England, the new church was to begin their conversion in taste if not religion to an architectural language which looked to recent buildings in London for inspiration.

The Great Fire of 1666 had obliterated large parts of the city of London, so providing Sir Christopher Wren with the opportunity to design a whole range of new city churches in

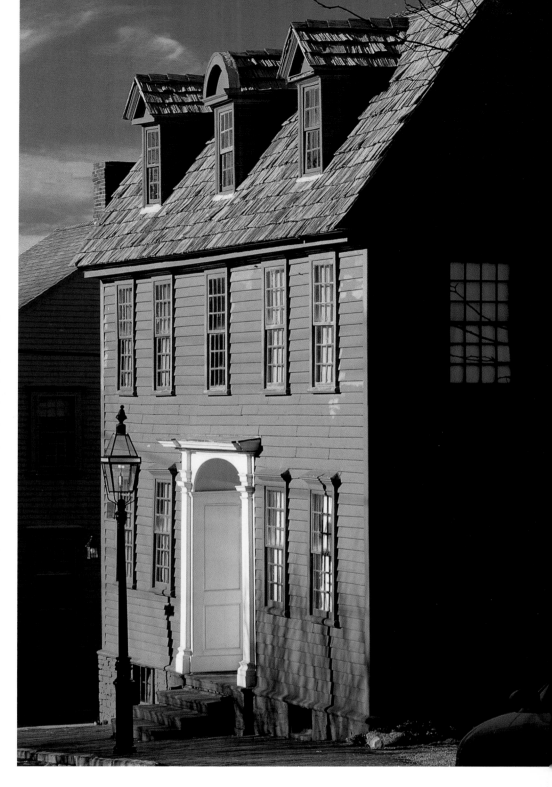

RHODE ISLAND

GEORGIAN IN NEWPORT

The second significant classical influence on architecture in the American colonies came from the Italian architect Andrea Palladio. His *Four Books* advocated a classicism based on a rigorous proportional system. In London Lord Burlington and William Kent published 14 editions of this influential treatise. Gentlemen and building tradesmen arriving in the colonies may have brought knowledge of, and enthusiasm for, the new Palladian classicism with them. But by far the most significant influence was the new populist literature they carried in their luggage.

From the 1730s a range of carpenters' handbooks, full of details of carved woodwork, doorways and cornices, were published, which provided practical guidance on Palladian design. Most popular were Batty Langley's unpretentious *The City and Country Builder* (1740) and *The Builder's Jewel* (1741), as well as William Salmon's *Palladio Londinensis* (1734).

The visual impact on Newport's domestic architecture was dramatic. Classical doorways, window and cornices were added to the traditional gambrel roofs. However, the standard building technique remained the heavy hand-hewn frame with notched and pegged joints. The only significant change before this point had been the general adoption (around 1700) of a layer of sheathing boards under the clapboarding. This double layer was warmer and much less draughty.

The Hunter House was built on Easton's Point overlooking the harbour from where the first two owners, the merchants Jonathon Nicholls Jnr and Colonel Joseph Wanton Jnr, could contemplate their respective profits. Nicholls's sophisticated tastes can still be seen in the finest remaining example of a panelled interior which survives from the mid-eighteenth century with winged heads of angels keeping watch over the alcoves, and, above them, wooden boxed cornices breaking forward over the pilasters.

LEFT Hunter House, Newport, 1748. Detail of garden façade. Classical wall and door details adorn a clapboarded wall
ABOVE John Bannister House, Newport, 1751

The Hunter House's fortunes, like those of the whole of Newport, were rocked by the American War of Independence. Wanton, a prominent Tory and thus loyal to the crown, was forced to flee in the face of French occupation after British forces withdrew in 1780. In his place came the French commander Admiral De Ternay, who promptly died in the house.

When British forces, under General Prescott, occupied the city, they had used as their headquarters the nearby Bannister House. This had been built in 1751 by John Bannister, a wealthy merchant whose household accounts indicated his heavy involvement in 'free trade' (i.e. smuggling). His large gambrel-roofed house included two interior chimneys and a spacious central hallway with a coved cornice.

During the British occupation the population fell from approximately nine to four thousand. When it was besieged by American forces, 480 wooden buildings were destroyed to satisfy the common need for firewood.

Newport was never to recover from the damage of the war and Providence eclipsed it as an economic centre. But what had emerged during the eighteenth century, in addition to the

LEFT Hunter House, seen from
the street. It looks directly onto
Newport harbour
BOTTOM LEFT Detail of drawing-
room panelling
ABOVE Dining room

nation's independence, was a truly metropolitan architecture
concerned not just with survival, but with matters of art and
learning, culture and taste.

NEW ENGLAND

THE SHAKERS

In 1774 Mother Anne Lee led eight members of the Society of Believers in Christ's Second Coming (or 'Shakers') away from religious persecution in England to start a new community in the New World. They lived in communities of the faithful that sought to be at once outside conventional society, and yet close enough to it to attract new believers. By the time of Anne's death in 1784 they had over ten settlements and several hundred members. These spiritual communities sought to draw strength from the practical goals of religious devotion, celibacy and intense communal labour.

By 1794, 11 self-contained villages had been established in New England according to Gospel Order, by which their members shared duties and property. The character of the wooden architecture they built reflected these particular communal needs.

The first buildings erected in the 1780s were meeting houses which provided the communities with places of worship and a sense of communal identity, but where the sexes were strictly segregated. Dance was an integral part of worship in which the sisters and brethren joined together. In time these dances had become more carefully ritualized and choreographed than the frenzied whirling and shaking that had given the Shakers their name.

The ground floor enclosed an unencumbered space for gatherings and dancing entered by two external doors, the right one for the sisters, the left for the brothers. A third door was provided for the ministry, the religious leaders who lived above the meeting space and who were segregated from the rest of the village to safeguard their superior spiritual purity.

Externally these buildings resembled the Anglo-Dutch architecture of the Hudson River Valley and southern Connecticut with their gambrel roofs, used in this case to accommodate the elders' living quarters. They were the only buildings painted white in accordance with the Shaker Rules of Millennial Law to distinguish their unique

symbolic and aspirational role leading the pursuit of heaven on earth. Consequently dwelling houses for the laity were modelled on them, albeit on a larger scale.

While Shaker buildings, by practical necessity, resembled the standard forms of contemporary structures, their greater communal scale often caused innovations in techniques which attracted a great deal of outside interest. The Round Barn at Hancock was widely celebrated. Originally built in 1826, it burned down in 1864 and was rebuilt with a circular loft and octagonal cupola supported by a central wooden frame.

ABOVE LEFT Round Barn, Hancock, Massachusetts, 1826, seen from the west
ABOVE & LEFT Roof structure. The different storeys served separate functions, the ground floor providing stabling for 52 cows

ABOVE Laundry and machine shop, Hancock, c.1790. The laundry building reflects Shaker belief in the supreme importance of order and cleanliness

Its form testifies to the sect's interest in efficiency and order. The structure is on two main levels, each accessed directly by earthen ramps. Hay was kept on the top floor where it could be tossed down by one of the brethren to the herd, kept on the perimeter of the floor beneath. Below, the cows' manure could be collected from the lowest level and taken to the fields. Despite the building's evident practical success, it remained the only one of its kind, as its plan was in strict contravention of ministry edicts which specified right angles and straight walls.

As with other Protestant groups, a central Shaker belief was

that constant work prevented idleness and hence sinfulness. Mother Anne implored them to 'put your hands to work and your hearts to God'. Separate workshops for sisters and brethren were built to manufacture goods for their own use and for sale.

Shaker products, like their architecture, reflect an intense concern with craftsmanship. Since the process of work brought one closer to God, the products of that work should reflect the sanctity of the experience. As Mother Anne admonished: 'Do all your work as though you had a thousand years to live, and as you would if you knew you must die tomorrow.' As a consequence,

ABOVE Meeting house, Hancock, 1793. First built for the Shaker village at Shirley, Massachusetts, it replaced the original Hancock meeting house which was pulled down in 1938. Both buildings were designed by Moses Johnson

TOP Sisters' dairy and weave shop, c.1793, with the brethren's workshop, c.1795, behind.

though their carpentry is plain and simple, their buildings are often beautifully proportioned and crafted. At the same time, the laundry building at Hancock illustrates how unprecious Shakers could be when converting their buildings.

The Shakers did not think of their buildings as permanent monuments. On the contrary, the beauty we find in them is a by-product of that utilitarian ideal which reflected the sanctity of the process of construction. They sought to build only the most perfect enclosure for worship and work – the twin requirements for heaven on earth.

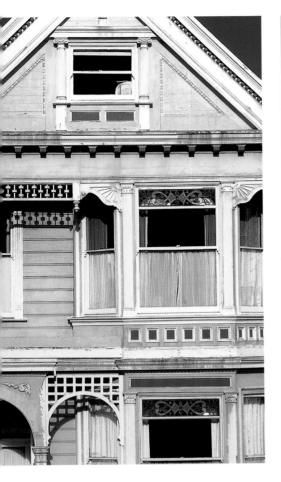

THE BUILDING BOOM

When gold was found in the northern Californian hills in 1849, a pueblo of huts and shacks called Yerba Buena became transformed into the city of San Francisco in the space of a few decades. During the peak period of the 1880s and 1890s, more than 1,500 people were involved in the city's development. Construction started on at least four new buildings a day as cable-car lines were extended further into outlying areas.

This phenomenal growth was made possible by an abundant supply of coastal redwood. It was cheap, durable and resistant to termites and fire. At the same time, the development of power-driven jigsaws and lathes greatly increased the speed at which the wood could be worked. An efficient framing technique had been invented in Chicago in the 1830s, which used standard lumber sizes and machine-made wire nails to form efficient but seemingly insubstantial structures nicknamed balloon frames. The flexibility of the frame was believed to be able to survive earthquakes and allowed space for plenty of glass in a climate without serious extremes of temperature.

Despite the speed of development, the houses of San Francisco show a huge variety in style and richness of detail. The houses of the 1870s followed an 'Italianate style' influenced by European and East Coast masonry architecture. The comparatively rudimentary milling machinery of the 1870s allowed for only a simple treatment of the façades, with flat window hoods and squeezed pediments. At the top, a bracketed cornice acted as a false front hiding the pitched roof behind.

During the 1880s, as millwrights became adept at producing complicated details quickly, prevailing styles changed. One article in 1875 presciently set the tone for the designs of the next decade. W.N. Lockington wrote in the *Overland Monthly* that: 'The wooden houses lie, like a man with a false shirt front – they try to hide their material… A wooden building should not ape a stone one, but should show its material and delight in it.'

The San Francisco 'stick style' of the 1880s had a much more explicit structure as reminiscent of Gothic as of classical architecture. Less effort was spent trying to reproduce classical details in wood such as quoins or Corinthian capitals. Instead, architects were presented with catalogues full of an

ABOVE & LEFT Queen Anne row houses, 712–22 Steiner Street, San Francisco, built in 1894–95 by contractor Matthew Kavanaugh

RIGHT Haas-Lilienthal House, San Francisco, 1886, by the architect Peter Schmidt. Interior of dining room **ABOVE** Window of circular tower room

assortment of details, including waffles, drips, leaves, sunbursts and geometric strips.

Façades were covered with this mass-produced wooden embellishment and painted, for the first time, in a whole gamut of colours. The result was a huge array of exuberant eclecticism, most of it straight out of a catalogue. As the *San Francisco Chronicle* noted, in 1887, there were 'houses with no two sides alike, houses of chaste and rigid outline, and houses all angles and florid garniture, houses eccentric and scrappy as a crazy quilt apparently pieced together from the leavings of other houses'.

In the 1890s architectural styles changed again. This is attributed, at least partially, to a competition held in 1884 by the *California Architect and Building News* to design a new San Francisco residence. Several hundred entries were received, nearly all from architects of the East Coast. The four winners had similar ideas. They envisaged an architecture of towers and steep gabled roofs with attic spaces behind them. Frieze bands and cornices replaced the vertical bands of the 1880s with a new horizontal emphasis. The developers wholeheartedly embraced the new style, though they often left out the costly towers. Today more of these Queen Anne-style houses survive than any other.

One particularly fine example of the style is the Haas-Lilienthal House of 1886. Its asymmetrical façade has projecting window bays and steep gable ends, and pivots around a circular shingled corner tower. This particular amalgamation of motifs is California's own, but its general character also forms part of an international phenomenon, variously known as the stick style, 'carpenter Gothic' and 'Swiss style', whose origins lie in the potent combination of cheap softwood, power-driven saws and the principle of mass production.

HOTEL DEL CORONADO

This monumental wooden edifice was the brainchild of Elias Babcock Jnr, a railway magnate who had been forced to retire through ill health and had moved to San Diego's sunny climate. Perhaps an awareness of his own mortality hastened Babcock's decision-making. He went into business with fellow retiree Hampton L. Story, bought the whole Coronado peninsula and the pair set about building a hotel, at a breakneck pace. Short of time rather than money, he ordered it to be 'constructed, furnished and conducted regardless of expense'. The Hotel del Coronado opened to guests on 19 February 1888, only 11 months after work had commenced on site.

The architects were three brothers: James, Merrit and Watson Reid. Babcock knew of their work designing huge timber railway sheds. Their experience of large-scale timber structures would prove invaluable as, for reasons of speed, the whole hotel had to be built out of 'green' (i.e. unseasoned) timber. To control the effect of shrinkage as the timber dried, the Reids used balloon framing, which requires pieces of timber two or more storeys in height. This was employed instead of the more economic 'platform' framing where each storey is constructed in turn, one above the other. Platform framing is very sensitive to shrinkage in the timbers' length as the floor timbers are used to project out to support the wall members.

Trees tall enough to make the balloon frame were only available in the northern Californian redwood forests. These were chained together into great rafts and floated down the Californian coast. A semi-skilled workforce of several hundred, mostly recruited from San Francisco's Chinatown, processed the logs into lumber on site. They were instructed to build the least complicated north façade first. They learned on the job, and managed to install three thousand window frames and doors, and hand-lay an estimated two million shingles.

To combat the threat of fire in such an enormous structure, the Reids invested in technological innovation. The hotel

became the first in the world to use electric lighting, installed by Thomas Edison himself. A notice in the rooms explained: 'This room is equipped with Edison electric light. Do not attempt to light with a match… the use of electricity for lighting is in no way harmful to health, nor does it affect the soundness of sleep.'

'The Del', as it is now known, has featured widely in American cultural life. Perhaps most memorably it provided Marilyn Monroe, Tony Curtis and Jack Lemmon with a fictional Florida resort in Billy Wilder's *Some Like It Hot*.

ABOVE LEFT Hotel del Coronado, San Diego. Courtyard façade. The building was planned around a big Spanish-style courtyard garden, 46m (150ft) wide by 76m (250ft) long

ABOVE The entrance façade is a fantastical mixture of gables, balconies and windows, culminating in a huge turreted corner tower above the ballroom

THE SHINGLE STYLE

McKim, Mead and White were among a large group of architects who found the inspiration for an entirely new architectural style in America's timber-framed heritage. Just as the English Arts and Crafts movement had drawn inspiration from Tudor and Elizabethan wood, so their American counterparts looked again at the seventeenth-century houses of Massachusetts Bay and the eighteenth-century architecture of Rhode Island.

McKim toured Rhode Island in the early 1870s. Then, with his friends Mead, White and Biglow, he went on a walking tour of New England specifically to study the early timber houses. There they probably visited several, like the Hoxie House on Cape Cod, which were entirely shingle-clad.

At the same time the English architect Richard Norman Shaw was designing houses of great originality clearly inspired by Tudor architecture. These combined expansive plans centred on large medieval-style hallways. They had half-timbered upper storeys and gable roofs. His houses, such as Leyes Wood and Hopedene, were profiled in both British journal *Building News* and *American Architect and Building News* to great critical acclaim.

Another influence upon American architecture was the discovery of Japanese architecture after Japan became open to trade in 1854. The World's Fair exhibition which followed profiled Japanese wooden architecture and excited great public interest. In both cases the new medium of photography was influential in providing a source of compelling new images to disseminate these ideas.

While architects were being exposed to a broader cultural range, changes were also taking place in American society that would provide them with a new breed of client. America's industrial development during the later nineteenth century had both created great wealth and placed it in the hands of a new generation of urban professionals. These men were rich enough to indulge in leisure time and were unencumbered by prejudices about how this time could or should be spent.

Newport, languishing for so long as an urban backwater, had retained its good looks and received a fresh stimulus as a playground for the East Coast rich. The Newport Casino

BELOW Newport Casino, Newport, Rhode Island, 1879–81. The club has a symmetrical façade along Bellevue Avenue with matching flattened gables, which conceal an informal asymmetrical arrangement within

was designed practically on a whim for publisher James Gordon Bennett, who, irritated by the stuffy atmosphere of the existing gentlemen's club, chose to open his own. His friends followed him to what became the centrepiece of Newport's recreational life and the first 'shingle style' building by the newly formed firm of Messrs McKim, Mead and White.

Bennett's brother-in-law, Isaac Bell, became another archetypal 'shingle style' client. He had both inherited money and personally amassed a fortune trading in cotton, retiring rich at the age of 31.

His house reflects an insouciant air of confident informality. The loose massing belies a sense of carefully studied geometry, the intention being to impart a sense of happy accident while leaving nothing to chance. The exterior displays various historical references. The broad gables recall the sides of Newport's eighteenth-century town houses. The small panes of glass recall the eighteenth-century glazing bars rather than contemporary windowpanes. But the ground floor is conceived as a radical series of organi-

cally connected spaces, which flow diagonally into each other through huge sliding doors, a clear reference to Japanese partitioning. Throughout, there are exquisite wooden details of complex derivation. There is evidence of Egyptian and Islamic influences, as well as of Norman Shaw and Henry Hobson Richardson.

The freedom of plan and form in the Isaac Bell House and the visual texture of continuous shingles were to prove extremely influential. Young architects who trained at the burgeoning firm of McKim, Mead and White absorbed their principles while architectural magazines across the country disseminated the designs of the office.

ABOVE LEFT Isaac Bell House, Newport, Rhode Island, 1881–83. Grand staircase
ABOVE MIDDLE Detail of fireplace and bay window in Mrs Bell's bedroom
ABOVE RIGHT Seen from the driveway, it appears loose and asymmetrical, disguising its tightly ordered plan

THE GAMBLE HOUSE

'Rich manufacturer will erect a palace – Ivory soap man to build' ran a headline in a local Pasadena newspaper in 1908. The manufacturer was David B. Gamble of Proctor and Gamble. But his building was destined to disappoint. Gamble built not a palace but a modest timber-framed house covered with shingles, which sat low to the ground with a delicate relationship to its garden reminiscent of Japanese houses.

It represented the ultimate expression of the aesthetic values of its creators, the architects Charles and Henry Greene. These brothers originally trained at the Manual Training School of Washington University, where the principal, Calvin Milton Woodward, taught practical building skills alongside design. 'The Cultured Mind, the Skilful Hand' ran a headline in the school's catalogue. Woodward was an avid reader of the writings of the founder of England's Arts and Crafts movement, William Morris. He responded to Morris's concern – that the Industrial Revolution was depriving man of the pleasure of a creative relationship with his work, that 'a certain sacredness in handicraft' had been lost. Thus, for Woodward, there was both a moral and an intellectual benefit to crafting objects.

The Greenes were ideal pupils. When the English architect C.S. Ashbee travelled across the United States, he enthused about the quality of their workmanship in a letter home. But the Greenes were also able to recognize the worth of truly gifted carpenters such as the Swedish brothers Peter and John Hall. They would use the technical precision of great craftsmen to feed their fascination with the minutiae of construction.

After a single meeting with David Gamble, the Greenes were commissioned. Gamble felt sufficiently confident to take his family on holiday while the house was being built. The result is a masterpiece of carpentry, which illustrates the Greenes' twin concerns of total design and exquisite

ABOVE The front door which incorporates leaded art-glass depicting the Tree of Life **BELOW** Detail of balcony, with joinery reminiscent of Japanese structural articulation

ABOVE The Gamble House,
Pasadena, 1908. The loose
massing of the garden façade
is integrated with a rock garden of Japanese inspiration

craftsmanship. Their drawings delineate an entirely original design for every single element in a room: panelling,
furniture, light fittings, even the images on carpets and
stained glass.

It is thought probable that the Greenes visited the
World's Columbian Exposition in Chicago in 1893. Here
they would have seen examples of Japanese buildings, an
architecture that had always answered Woodward's strin-
gent criteria. Its influence on the Greenes was clear but
never explicit. The lucid expression of timber construction
in the Gamble House follows Japanese precedent without
aping it. The overall visual effect, rather than strict structural economy, is paramount, so timbers may be larger
than they need to be. As Henry Greene observed, their aim
was to 'make the whole as direct and simple as possible, but
always with the beautiful in mind as the final goal'. Hence
timbers are shaped and finished with their ends tapered
to soften their visual impact. This is particularly clear in
the large porches, which overhang the ground floor to the
north and west, and in the attic storey above.

ABOVE Ceiling of attic storey,
showing king post trusses
with expressed mortice-and-
tenon. Oregon pine
RIGHT Detail of piano case
fitted into the living-room
wall panel

From the street façade the north porch balances the much more familiar domestic gable-end to the south. From the garden, the heavily timbered and bracketed porches interfere, creating a picturesque effect. The attic storey roof is supported by two substantial king post trusses of Oregon pine (a wood chosen for its straight grain and purity from defect) with the mortise-and-tenon joints exposed.

The interior of the Gamble House responds as completely as any domestic space to William Morris's dictum to 'have nothing in your house that you do not know to be useful or believe to be beautiful'. Immediately inside the front door is an alcove created by the dogleg of the staircase. The monumental timber wall is a structural expression of the risers behind, reinforced by beautifully rounded corbels and the rhythmic pattern of railings above. This language of carefully moulded timber beams is continued in the living room. Here Burmese teak trusses, with gracefully curved queen posts, surround the fireplace inglenook. This zone is continued around the room with carved redwood panels inspired by Japanese *rammas* illustrating scenes of nature. These contrast with lighter walls in Burmese teak veneer.

Every detail of the furniture is co-ordinated. All side-board doors and cabinets are built in to the walls and fashioned from the same Honduras mahogany. Even the freestanding piano is sheathed in a tailor-made mahogany casing which had to be specially shipped to Cincinnati for the piano to be fitted before it could be integrated into the living-room wall.

Throughout, it is the practical details of wood construction, given precision handcrafting, that provide the Gamble House with its decorative richness. Even the stained glass of the front door depicts a tree. More than just a symbol of the carpenter's timber, it seems to pay homage to the glory of the Californian landscape as a whole.

CHAPTER SIX

SOUTH-EAST ASIA

The term 'South-East Asia' is here used to describe the peninsula that lies to the south of the tropic of Cancer and then extends further south into the Indonesian archipelago. It is bordered to the west and north by the ancient and influential civilizations of India and China, from which its sobriquet 'Indo-China' derives. It is from these neighbours that first Hinduism and then Buddhism have spread across the region, bringing with them influential artistic and architectural traditions.

One common feature of the region is the heat. On the peninsula itself the annual temperatures remain around 27°C (80.6°F), with a wet season from around May to October which delivers an average of 120–200cm (47–78in) of rain a year. To the south, annual temperatures rise and seasonal variations diminish closer to the equator. This climate has resulted in a landscape of densely packed tropical and monsoonal forests that, despite the best efforts of man, still dominate the terrain. Half of Thailand, 60 per cent of Laos

and 75 per cent of Cambodia are still forested. The Indonesian peninsula was still densely forested as recently as 1950: 40 per cent of what remained in 1950 was cleared in the following 50 years. Nevertheless, the Indonesian forest remains the largest in Asia, and the third largest forest on the planet.

These forests have supplied an abundance of exceptionally strong, durable wood suitable for building, especially teak, mahogany and rosewood. The most commonly used, and greatly prized, is teak (*tectona grandis*). This grows to a height of 30m (98ft) over a period of 60 to 80 years, with its main balks of timber being about 18m (59ft) long with 2m (6½ft) girths. It is a moderately hard wood impervious to changes in moisture and temperature. Its oil content repels insects and fungal attack. Because of the heaviness and high specific gravity of green teak the tree is often felled three years after 'girdling' (i.e. chopping away the bark and part of the sapwood). During this interval it loses enough moisture to be more easily worked. Teak timber

can be air-seasoned quickly and provides strength, elasticity and endurance.

The varied inhabitants of South-East Asia often have a high degree of expertise in the construction of timber frames. There are almost as many house styles as there are ethnic groups to build them.

Another universal feature is that houses are built on piles or posts that lift the floor of the building off the ground. This seems to have three main functions: to alleviate the effects of flooding in a tropical climate; to diminish the threat posed by animals and snakes; and to improve ventilation and make maximum use of the prevailing breezes.

A final common denominator is that construction in South-East Asia is a social and religious activity. House-building requires the gathering together of a large group of people to erect the frames in a sequence determined by custom. It also necessitates a negotiation with the spirit world. This might involve the performance of religious ceremonies during construction (as in Thailand) or in respecting the continued presence of long-dead ancestors (as in Indonesia).

ABOVE Wat Yai, Samut Songkhram, Thailand. Scripture repositories were traditionally placed above ponds of water to protect the sacred contents from ants, termites and fire **LEFT** The Bale Kambang, or 'Floating Pavilion', Indonesia **FAR LEFT** Wat Si Rong Muang, built by Burmese immigrants near Lampang, Thailand. Ceremonial doorways open onto a veranda

ABOVE The Viharn Lei Kham of Wat Phra Singh, Chang Mai, after 1345, has 'Buddha's eyebrows': arched spandrel panels that align with the image of the Buddha inside
RIGHT Lanna's *viharn*, built without outer walls, rely upon low sweeping roofs for protection
FAR RIGHT In Lampang the Viharn Luang, 1476, shelters a gilded brick *ku* which enshrines the principal Buddha image

THE LANNA THAI WAT

Lanna, which literally means 'a million rice fields', was an independent northern Thai kingdom, protected from Siamese Thailand to the south by a range of heavily forested mountains. It had a loose political structure which allowed artists a greater degree of autonomy than the other Thai states. Lanna's rich forests also provided abundant supplies of teak wood of exceptional quality for sculpting and building.

Lanna artists drew upon Indian, Sri Lankan, and neighbouring Burmese and Laotian influences to create an artistic and architectural tradition that was distinctive yet full of regional variation. The focus of their efforts was the centrepiece of Thai religious practice, the *wat*. There is no word in English that accurately conveys the meaning of this Thai term. It is applied to all walled religious enclosures in Thailand, whatever their size. Very often the enclosure functions as a temple, and more often than not contains a monastery, although neither's presence is guaranteed. Throughout Thailand the *wat*'s principal buildings are constructed from wooden frames, supporting tiers of roofs culminating in stepped gables, with each lower tier flaring out at a shallower angle. In Lanna, these have a distinctively squat appearance caused by their wider girth and roofs that reach down almost to the ground. The *viharn*, or preaching hall, is also given pre-eminence over the *ubosot*, or assembly hall, both in size and position.

The finest example in the capital, Chang Mai, is the Viharn Lei Kham of Wat Phra Singh, which was originally built after 1345 but was then heavily renovated in the first decade of the nineteenth century. It shows archetypal Lanna style – low walls and sweeping roof lines, terminating in roof finials called *cho fa* or 'sky clusters', which represent a garuda bird in a *cho fa pak krut* (garuda beak finial). The front façade shows another

ABOVE The interior Viharn
Lei Kham of Wat Phra Singh,
Chang Mai, is covered with
traditional gilding

RIGHT The outer columns of the
Viharn Luang were replaced with
concrete in a disappointing
1830 restoration

distinctive Lanna feature – the *kong khieu*, or 'Buddha's eyebrows': arched spandrel panels linking the red lacquered portico posts and aligning with the image of the Buddha inside. On either side, smaller 'Buddha's eyebrows' echo the centre which are also called 'bird wing gables' (*na ban pik nok*).

Other types of *viharn* unique to Lanna are those constructed without outer walls, relying upon roofs reaching close to the ground to shelter their Buddha images from the elements. One of the most exceptional examples is the Viharn Luang from Wat Phra That Lampang Luang. This *wat*, whose name means

the 'Great Relic Wat of Lampang', derives its significance from the legend that the Buddha came to Lampang and donated a tuft of his hair. Here the *viharn*, which dates from 1476, has been placed at the centre of the compound and houses a spectacular gilded brick *ku* enshrining the *wat*'s principal Buddha image. It is protected by a colossal, and beautifully proportioned, three-tiered roof.

Unfortunately, the combination of rich natural resources and influential neighbours resulted in a troubled political history for Lanna. The Burmese invaded in the sixteenth century,

capturing Chang Mai in 1558, and ruled Lanna for the next two hundred years. They were only unseated in 1776 with the assistance of the Siamese who, in turn, promptly took control. The following century, the British Empire conquered Burma, creating a unified Thailand, forcing the Siamese to concede access to supplies of Lanna's teak.

During the period of Burmese control, the Burmese respected Lanna's Buddhist inheritance for their own religious reasons rather than any general sense of benevolence (they had razed the Siamese city of Ayutthaya to the ground). As a result, these conquests contributed new examples to Lanna's rich architectural heritage, with Burmese and later Burmese-British architecture.

BURMA

BURMA

THE BURMESE MONASTERY

The forests of Burma contained a great wealth of high-quality teak wood. The designation of teak as a royal monopoly from which state revenues were derived indicated its particular importance. But as the kings of Burma also acted as 'defenders of the Buddhist faith' they made supplies available for the construction of wooden monasteries throughout the country. These foundations were supplemented by the widespread practice of private individuals establishing monasteries in order to accrue spiritual merit for themselves.

It seems likely that the type of Burmese wooden monastery that survives to this day, the *hpon-gyi kyanung*, evolved originally from Burma's indigenous domestic architectural tradition, albeit with some features of Indian origin. These are large teak buildings, constructed on wooden platforms supported on pillars, which use a method of construction which probably dates back to Neolithic times, before the advent of Buddhism in Burma. This system employs beams inserted through the vertical pillars to cross-brace and support the floors, the walls and the ceilings. The pillars in the centre of the structure run right up to support the ridge beam, perhaps 20m (65ft) from the ground, while those on the periphery rise no higher than perhaps 3 or 4m (10–13ft).

The form and layout of the typical Burmese monastery reflect monastic practice in Burma, where, unlike in Thailand, all the various functions are accommodated in a single structure. A long platform built on parallel rows of pillars supports places for prayer, preaching, accommodation, instruction and sometimes a library-museum.

One of the most noticeable features of Indian derivation is the *pyatthat hsaung*. This is the tallest part of the structure and is often crowned by a tall spire made of multi-tiered roofs. The word *pyatthat* derives from the Sanskrit word *prasada*, referring to a multi-tiered pavilion whose shape was based on Mount Meru, the mountain lying at the apex of the universe in Hindu/Buddhist cosmology. As such the spires of Burma share a similar lineage to the Meru structures of the Indonesian island of Bali.

A central pillar anchored to a substantial tie beam running between the main pillars supports the spires. Each roof layer sits upon rafters supported by an internal frame and hidden by elaborately carved spandrel panels. The spire is surmounted by a distinctive finial whose complex form combines rings of lotus leaves, a 'banana bud' (*ngyet-pyaw-hpu*) and 'onion head' (*kyet-thun-khaung*) forms. Above these, crowns of iron support the vane.

RIGHT An angel-like *deva* figure overlooks mortal and immortal figures on a monastery at Nyaung U, Pagan
ABOVE LEFT The treasure room below the *pyatthat hsaun*
ABOVE RIGHT The multi-tiered roofs of a *pyatthat hsaun*

The *pyatthat hsaung* is used to house sacred texts and images of the Buddha as well as serving as a private chapel for the monks. In recognition of this special purpose, its floor is usually raised to a higher lever than anywhere else in the building, accessed by a series of stairs (usually three) on one or more sides. The *pyatthat hsaung* is linked to the main chambers of the monastery by the *sanu-hsuang*, where the abbot resides. If there is no separate library, this is used to house manuscript chests full of palm-leaf books. Beyond this, the main space, or *marabin hsaung*, is divided by a transverse partition into two halls. The first,

which contains another Buddha image, is shared by monks and laymen for preaching and prayer, the second serves ceremonies performed by the monastic community alone. Beyond the main halls lies the storage hall (*baw-ga hsuang*), which has the lowest roof height: there is a hierarchical sequence beginning with the *pyatthat hsaung* at the other end of the building.

Outside, Burmese monasteries are saturated with decorative carved ornamentation. Tradition decreed that their roofs should be used to portray the 22 layers of heaven that surround the summit of Mount Meru. Consequently their gables, eaves and ridges are covered with flame-like finials and sculptures of people and mythical creatures.

The ground floor of the building contains didactic examples of Buddhist folklore to assist in the instruction of novices. Thus sculptures illustrate Buddhist 'Jakata' stories with scenes from everyday life. Below the balustrades are carvings of mythical and demonic creatures. In Burmese Buddhist cosmology humans occupy the space between the upper and lower worlds and should try to derive strength from both. Hence, angel-like *deva* figures from the celestial world and ugly *ogre* figures from the lower world are often carved on either side of

ABOVE A single structure provides accommodation, and areas for study and instruction, prayer and services with the lay community

ABOVE LEFT The *marabin hsaung*, the main space of the monastery, is divided by a transverse partition into two halls. The chamber beyond the partition is solely for the use of the monks

ABOVE The *pyatthat hsaung* of Wat Chong Kham, seen from the unusually asymmetrically placed *marabin hsaung*
RIGHT Roof of a *marabin hsaung*

entranceways, where they serve to guard the monastery together.

Burmese monasteries are not only confined to Burma: Shan Burmese immigrants built a number in Lanna. One of the earliest is the eighteenth-century Wat Chong Kham, originally located in the village of Ngao in the western hills of Lampang province, but now in Muang Boren, Samut Prakhan. These monasteries were unpainted and have only external decoration. The delicacy of the decorated bargeboards and roof shingles is offset by the flat wall surfaces. Later on, during the nineteenth century, the Shan monasteries received a great deal

more decoration, with richly coloured interiors featuring gilding, coloured glass and mosaic work such as those at Wat Si Rong Muang near Lampang. They also went on to embrace corrugated iron as an alternative to traditional shingled roofs.

When Burma was colonized by the British in 1885, there were thought to be at least 15,000 monasteries in the country, or around two per village. But the British viewed them ambivalently. James Fergusson's influential *History of Indian and Eastern Architecture* (1876) concluded: 'However dazzling [their] splendour, such barbaric magnificence is worthy only of a half civilised

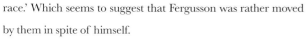

ABOVE Two *pyatthat hsaung* adorn the profile of Wat Si Chum, 1892, the biggest Burmese temple in Thailand
LEFT & ABOVE LEFT A series of buddhas surround the *sanu-hsuang*, where the abbot resides in Wat Chong Kham

race.' Which seems to suggest that Fergusson was rather moved by them in spite of himself.

Because these monasteries remained in the custody of their abbots, they were not included in the Archaeological Survey of India's 'Protected Monuments' list and many fell into a state of disrepair. Changes in Burmese society and the fact that Burmese Buddhists believe an individual does not accumulate merit by refurbishing the works of others have left these buildings in jeopardy. Consequently wooden monasteries have been in decline in Burma for well over a hundred years. Thousands have been destroyed.

THAILAND

THE THAI HOUSE

The traditional Thai house has an ancient lineage. Houses featuring steep tapered gabled roofs hovering above the ground on raised platforms appear in Dvaravati stone reliefs of the eighth century. Indeed, houses supported by posts appear on bronze drums of the Dong Son culture in Vietnam between the fourth century BC and the first century AD. It is plausible that a continuous tradition has existed from then until the present day.

The form of the house derives from an eminently intelligent response to the tropical climate. The roof pitch is steep to reduce the risk of rain leaking through the palm-leaf thatch or shingles. The eaves greatly overhang the main structure, thereby reducing the risk of saturation in tropical downpours, and protecting the occupants from the hot sun. The raised terrace similarly combats flooding with large gaps between its members designed to dry the floor out swiftly after showers. The walls of a Thai house taper inwards to give the structure greater wind-bracing as well as making the attachment of the walls simpler as they can be leant against the posts while being jointed together.

The house was also a response to Thailand's predominantly rural society, with its system of extended families. When a Thai man married, he would go and live with his wife's family. A fresh structure would be built for the couple which was connected to the parent's house via a raised terrace courtyard.

Windows, both on to the terrace and outside, ensured cross-ventilation. If necessary, the entire extended family could dismantle their houses, move and reassemble them elsewhere.

The process of building houses reflected Thai beliefs about the power of the natural world and the delicacy of man's relationship with it. Careful astrological consultation would determine an auspicious day for the house to be erected. On the eve of the assigned day, a ceremony was held to ask the spirit of the site for permission to build there. The correct time was calculated for the positioning of the two primary house posts, and their

ABOVE Thai houses are made up of a series of interconnected structures which accommodate an extended family group
ABOVE RIGHT Garuda finials adorn both secular and temple architecture
BOTTOM RIGHT Gables are often adorned with elaborately carved boards
BOTTOM FAR RIGHT The Jim Thompson House, Bangkok, is made up of a number of 18th- and 19th-century Thai houses

placement again accompanied by a ceremony. Only wood of exceptional quality was used for these posts, reflecting symbolic as well as practical concerns.

The conjunction of practical and astrological requirements is a consistent feature of Thai house design. Houses were built facing either north or east, with the bedrooms looking out in these directions because they were associated with rising power and success. They were also cooler. Entrance doors have raised thresholds in order to deter evil spirits (and, incidentally, reptiles and snakes) from entering the chambers, as well as strengthening the frame of the building.

Different trees are used for different parts of the building. Traditionally, the footings for the house posts are made of Indian coral wood because it is particularly resistant to rotting. The teak frame uses mortice-and-tenon joints which are further secured in place by wooden nails (*samae*) of blackwood driven through the joint. Inside the rooms the teakwood is commonly polished, but outside either it is left untouched or painted with a red creosote preservative first imported from Great Britain in the nineteenth century.

ABOVE The Jim Thompson House, Bangkok. The verandas and connecting corridors are enclosed, breaking with Thai tradition **LEFT** The entrance staircase **FAR LEFT** Jim Thompson's study

Some of the central ideas behind the Thai House were re-interpreted by the American architect and entrepreneur Jim Thompson in Bangkok in the 1960s. He bought six original Thai structures and re-erected an extended Thai family house, introducing various innovations of his own. Thompson's main 'drawing-room' house was originally built around 1800 and was occupied by several generations of a weaving family in the village of Bang Krua (later swallowed up by Bangkok). Eager to be able to better appreciate the decorative wall panels, Thompson re-erected the structure with the walls reversed so that their decoration was visible from the inside. Around it he connected a further five house units sourced from southern Thailand and dating from the early nineteenth century to 1918. Rather than arranging his house units around an open terrace, Thompson used the drawing-room house as his core. The other houses were directly connected to it in an H-shaped plan. The house was filled with Western furniture and Thompson's spectacular collection of Thai art.

Despite his scrupulous adherence to Thai ritual in his house's construction, Thompson disappeared in very inauspicious circumstances, while travelling in the Cameron Highlands of Malaysia in 1967.

ABOVE The Jim Thompson
House, Bangkok. In order to
enjoy the decorative wall
panels, Thompson reversed the
walls of the drawing-room house
ABOVE LEFT Thompson filled
his house with an extensive
collection of Thai art
LEFT Carving of a Thai prince in
the Thompson House

BALI

DIRECTIONAL TEMPLES

The Hindu and Buddhist faiths at one time dominated western Indonesia. The great stone monuments of Borobudur and Prambanan on Java testify to their influence. However, the rise of Islam in the fifteenth century threatened Hindu dynasties right across the archipelago. The reigning Hindu Majapahit dynasty, who had ruled Java since 1292, retreated to Bali at the beginning of the sixteenth century. Here their religious beliefs were assimilated into a strong native animist tradition to produce an idiosyncratic version of Hinduism unique to Bali.

The Balinese cosmology reflects the island's volcanic topography. It defines the human world as literally a middle ground between the world of demons inhabiting the ocean and the mountainous realm of gods and ancestors. Buttressing this self-sufficient worldview is the belief that the Indian Mount Meru (or Mahameru), the notional centre of the universe in the Hindu faith, was moved to Bali to become its highest volcanic peak, Gunung Agung.

All buildings on Bali are orientated along a path between the mountains and the sea in order to properly position man in relation to the spirit world. Central to this process are the island's temples (*pura*). These are specifically defined as 'places where the gods occasionally visit'. And, as such, the favour of the gods must be maintained by providing offerings and observing rituals at the site.

There are over 20,000 temples on Bali, not including the innumerable private temples within house compounds. There are temples for the worship of village ancestors, for the dead in general, for the spirits of lakes, and for communal worship with other members of a whole principality. All these temples share a similar general form, comprising a series of walled

LEFT *Meru* at Pura Besakih, the holiest directional temple complex on the island, on the slopes of Gunung Agung
ABOVE Some of the wooden *meru* sit on stone bases, Pura Besakih

compounds, the innermost of which represents heaven. The focus for rituals are the shrines covered with graceful wooden structures made up of ascending layers of roofs thatched with sugar-palm leaves. Their name, *meru*, derives from the cosmic mountain Mount Meru. The base represents the earth and the storeys (*tumpang*) represent successive heavens (*swargaloka*). It is via these layers of celestial dwelling that the deity occasionally descends to earth.

The most important temples on Bali are the nine 'directional temples' (*kayangan jagat*), which have been built at important geographical positions such as the mountains, overlooking the sea and by important lakes. They form a network that helps protect the whole population of Bali. At the centre of the network is Pura Besakih, the most important temple complex on the

island, which is located on the slopes of Gunung Agung. It contains 22 separate temples including Pura Penataran Agung, the mother temple of Bali where all Balinese are free to worship. The complex includes 170 shrines and sub-temples for each of the eight sections of the island (now known as *kabupaten*) and a further 18 individual sanctuaries for different groups. There are 50 *merus* in total, all orientated along their central axis with the summit of Gunung Agung.

THE WATER PAVILIONS OF TAMAN GILI

When the Majapahit removed to Java they established their cultural and political centre in Klungkung, a small town in the shadow of Gunung Agung. In 1685 it became the capital, and while not the most powerful city on the island it remained the seat of justice and played a major role for over 500 years in the politics of the island.

The Dutch bombarded the city in 1908. All that survives today are fragments of the great wooden palace of Klungkung. These are two buildings dating from the eighteenth century which were part of the Taman Gili (or 'Island Garden') that once belonged to the palace.

The Consultation Pavilion for Peace and Prosperity (Kerta Cosa) remained the seat of the supreme court up until the 1950s. This simple teak pavilion contained three gilded chairs where the judges sat, attended by lawyers and a scribe. On the ceiling above them, *wayang*-style murals depict the torture and destruction of the damned and the entrance into heaven of the worthy.

Nearby, the Floating Pavilion sits surrounded by a moat. It is an open-sided pavilion and has colourful ceiling paintings depicting scenes from the 'Sutasoma' legends. Sutasoma was a tantric Buddhist holy man who offered himself as food to a starving tigress in the place of her cubs, thereby demonstrating perfect altruism.

ABOVE The Bale Kambang or 'Floating Pavilion'
LEFT The ceiling of the Bale Kambang depicts scenes from the story of the Buddhist saint Sutasoma
FAR LEFT The Kerta Gosa was Bali's supreme court until 1950. Pictures on the ceilings depict the damnation of the guilty and the enlightenment of the worthy

THE SULAWESI HOUSE OF ORIGIN

Sulawesi is a large island to the north of Bali with a complex curving shape. Its southern mountains are populated by an ethnic group, the Toraja, whose traditional religion is known as Aluk to Dolo ('The Way of the Ancestors'). The central focus of religious practice is a wooden house tradition, the *Banua Toraja* or 'House of Origin'.

According to Toraja legend, they arrived on the shore of Sulawesi in boats from the north. Shipwrecked on the island,

they used their craft as roofs of shelters. From this the curious characteristic saddle-backed roof derives. Toraja houses are still built facing north in recognition of this direction of origin.

Tongkonan, as they are routinely called, are built on wooden piles. All the timber members are assembled by constructing complex prefabricated elements that slot ingeniously together without the use of nails. First, the heavy wooden piles are placed in the ground. Horizontal tie beams are placed into

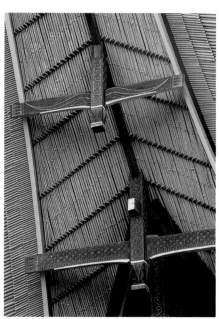

morticed timber posts carefully forked to provide immediate stability, before being slotted over other members.

Tying a series of ridgepoles on top of each other at one end creates the concave roof form. At the other end spars are placed between the ridgepoles, levering each end up into the air. External freestanding poles, connected to the roof by transverse ties, support the entire overhang. Rattan is used to tie bamboo poles on to the top of the rafters and the bamboo is then laid on top of these in tight waterproof layers.

The decoration of Toraja houses reflects their hierarchical society, and villagers are only permitted to adorn their homes with symbols deemed appropriate to their social class. Spiral designs and animal motifs may be painted, but only in red, white, yellow and black, which represent different festivals in the Toraja calendar. For the Toraja, the house serves as a symbol of family identity. Placentas from children born in the home must be buried on the east side of the house and, as a consequence, these flexible structures can never be moved. The placentas are believed to call children back when, as adults, they stray far from home.

The shape of the traditional houses of the Toraja people are said to derive from upturned boats. They are constructed using an ingenious mortice-and-tenon system which slots together without the use of nails

CHAPTER SEVEN

AUSTRALIA

In 1786 Lord Sydney, the Home Office minister, submitted the 'Heads of a Plan' to the British government proposing the foundation of a penal colony in 'New Holland' (as Australia was then known). This maintained that transporting prisoners would be 'reciprocally beneficial to themselves and the State'. It is now believed that one of the additional benefits to the state would be to satisfy the Royal Navy's urgent need to secure fresh sources of timber for ship-building. Defeat in the American War of Independence in 1783 had left Britain without access to American timber. A special House of Commons committee questioned explorers about the possible availability of wood in New Holland. Captain Cook was unhelpful, but the botanist Joseph Banks, who had accompanied Cook on his 1770 voyage, asserted that the timber 'appeared to me to be fit for all the purposes of house building and ship building'.

When the first ships reached Botany Bay the trees they found in great profusion were the Australian eucalypts that still make up 75 per cent of the trees of the continent. This varied group

of hardwoods grow in nearly all the climatic and geographical regions of the continent from swamps to the semi-desert. Some grow no taller than a metre, others over 80m (262ft). Colonists were at first dismayed at the type of timber provided by what they called the 'gum-tree'. Arthur Philips, the first governor, complained in his first despatch to Lord Sydney in May 1788 that 'the timber is well described in Captain Cook's voyage, but unfortunately it has one very bad quality, which puts it to great inconvenience; I mean the large gum-tree, which splits and warps in such a manner when used green, and to which necessity obliged us, that a store-house boarded up with this wood is rendered useless'.

In time the more favourable attributes of the eucalypts were discovered. The one species immediately appreciated was 'cedrela', or red cedar. First logged in 1790, it satisfied such a wide range of needs – fencing, house timbers, joinery, furniture – that resources were exhausted 90 years later. Other trees had more specific uses: red-gums could stand in water without rotting, making them ideal

TOP 1920s bathing boxes, near Dendy Street, Brighton, Melbourne

ABOVE The balustrades and screens of Rangemoor, 1910, by Robin Dods

for bridges, wharves and foundations; stringy-bark was cut for general construction and its bark was used for roofing; 'ironbarks' were so tough as to be initially impossible to use but they split into excellent shingles. Both stringy-bark and ironbark were astonishingly strong and, once seasoned, relatively incombustible. However, these ultra-hard hardwoods had a major drawback in that they did not float, making their transport very difficult.

The history of wooden architecture in Australia is, in large part, the story of the ambivalent attitude of the settlers to the native eucalypts whose attributes are to some extent only now being fully explored. Throughout this period the Australian softwoods, and those imported from other parts of the British Empire or the United States, remained an alternative source of timber. But while native Australian trees would be found to have many practical uses, Banks was proved wrong in one regard: they never satisfied the demands of shipbuilding.

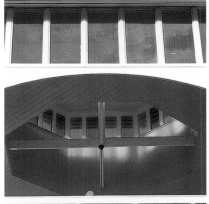

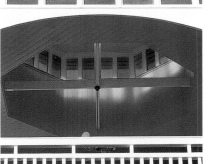

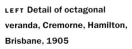

LEFT Detail of octagonal veranda, Cremorne, Hamilton, Brisbane, 1905

ABOVE Old timber conveyor belt in the new W Hotel bar of Woolloomooloo wharf, Sydney, 1910–16

GOLD-RUSH VERNACULAR

Gold was discovered in Australia in 1851. The richest strikes were in the newly created colony of Victoria to the north and west of Melbourne. Victoria's population, which had numbered 76,000 before the discovery, trebled in three years, reaching 540,000 in a decade. The burgeoning population was housed with the help of imported prefabricated houses. These were timber-framed and weatherboarded buildings which may have been derived from balloon-frame construction in California,

a technology that was already housing those caught up in the San Francisco Gold Rush. Much of the timber was certainly imported from the west coast of America (often Oregon pine), as well as from the Pacific Islands, the Far East and Tasmania.

However, Australian carpentry practice differed from the American balloon frame in a number of ways. The frame used was both lighter and stronger, using slim wooden cross-bracing, checked flush into the corners. The heavy corner posts used in

North American frames were not employed in Australia. Instead changes were made to corner jointing which allowed whole lengths of wall frame to be nailed together on the ground before being levered into position.

The same global financial forces that stimulated the Gold Rush provided the materials to house it. New products were imported from Great Britain. Here, machine-cut nails were manufactured at a rate of over 100,000 per machine per day. Galvanizing had been patented in London in 1837 and each year hundreds of tons of galvanized metal roofing arrived at the port of Melbourne. Another source for the Australian wooden house was the prefabricated house designs patented in London for the use of emigrants. These were in use right across the empire from India, South Africa and Sierra Leone to Australia. In 1830 John Manning marketed 'Portable Colonial Cottages'. Peter Thompson, a London builder and carpenter, also designed a flat-packed house which shows many similarities with Australian timber houses: stud-wall frames, sheathed in boarding and often including lean-to verandas. The construction of such houses was widely advertised in trade journals and newspapers. By 1850 Andrew Petrie's Brisbane firm was manufacturing portable buildings to take into Queensland's interior.

ABOVE, TOP & LEFT The wooden houses of St Kilda, Melbourne, are the inheritors of a timber tradition that swept Victoria during the Gold Rush

THE QUEENSLANDER

The most distinctive house type in Australia is not unique to the state, nor are its constituent elements unique to Australia. However, a particular combination of components, used in a limited number of ways, gives it an instantly recognizable appearance obviously suited to its subtropical environment. Yet it was not climatic conditions alone that determined the form of the 'Queenslander'.

Brisbane, unlike Melbourne, grew slowly at first. Free, for the time being, from gold-fever, land prices remained low, so that even the working classes could afford to purchase their own land. In 1860 the Queensland government sought to increase immigration by handing out land orders to the value of £18, hoping thereby to encourage farmers to settle inland. Many, however, simply stayed in Brisbane, using their land orders to purchase residential allotments. In 1885 the Undue Subdivision of Land Prevention Act determined that the minimum size of a residential allotment should be 16 perches (0.04 hectares/0.1 acres) so as to minimize the risk of fire spreading in a wooden city. Hence detached houses became the norm, even for the poor, and a predominantly suburban city was born. Wood, suitable for building, was in abundant supply along the Queensland coast. Indeed, the selection of sites for settlement was influenced by

the location of forests of softwoods, mainly hoop and bunya pine. Steam-powered sawmills first established in Brisbane in 1850 produced cheap timber components such as studs and boards. Later they would produce whole windows and doors. Timber would remain the cheapest building material until the 1950s.

These products were assembled into stud-frame houses. The light vertical studs 10x5cm (5x2in) in size were spaced along the perimeter at 45–60cm (18–24in) centres. They were typically tenoned and screw-nailed into the floor and ceiling plates. Diagonal cross-braces (2.5–5cm/1–2in diameter) were then worked flush with the inside face of the studs. In a technique peculiar to Queensland only the inside face of the frame was sheathed with a single layer of chamfer boards. This economy exposed the frame in an echo of Western European half-timbering. It was only possible because of Queensland's exceptionally mild winters; otherwise the exposed frames would have rotted.

The entire Queenslander was typically raised from the ground on stumps. There are various explanations for this. In

ABOVE The veranda of Rangemoor, 1910, has an undulating bressummer with fretwork decoration typical of the solid style of Robin Dods

RIGHT Ralahyne, 1888, by G.H.M. Addison, has a veranda supported by pairs of thin timber posts reminiscent of the international stick style

ABOVE The Ipswich Club, 1898. A grand divided stair and octagon established the social pretensions of the squatter settlement of Ipswich as it threatened to eclipse Brisbane RIGHT Glentworth, Rosalie, 1880s, has the classic surrounding verandas with delicate posts of the original Queenslanders

ABOVE Boondah, Rosalie, 1907, shows the motifs imported at the beginning of the century: Indian-style roof, ventilated roof gables and Art Nouveau-influenced stained glass

divided on the axis by a corridor with large façade-length verandas. The veranda was a feature derived from Indian architecture that had been imported into Britain by returning colonists. George Eliot registered its social pretensions in the novel *Daniel Deronda* (1876) when Gwendolyn Harleth says of Grandcourt: 'He has all the qualities that would make a husband tolerable – battlements, veranda, stables.' But the veranda proved to have legitimate practical benefits in the hot Queensland sun and became a defining feature of the house. Sometimes it was highly decorated with cast-iron balustrade panels and rhythmic double-timber posts such as at Ralahyne of 1888.

Roofs were steeply pitched to increase the volume of air acting as insulation in the attic space. Large gabled ventilators were often built into the apex of hipped roofs to allow hot air to escape. Inlets in the eaves' linings and outlets near the ridge also helped aerate the room.

After Australia's federation in 1901 a 'Federation style' swept the nation. The success of Queensland's wooden tradition can be gauged by the limited headway made by the new style in the state. To some extent this was because Queensland was decentralized and remote, and ideas took longer to be adopted, but mainly it was because it was essentially a masonry style, which did not satisfy the demands of Queensland's climate as successfully as the timber tradition.

Some Queenslanders did, however, reveal stylistic influences from foreign architecture. The cupola domes of

Brisbane it was probably encouraged by the undulating topography, which would otherwise have incurred costly levelling of the ground before building. Elsewhere it would have helped prevent the spread of termites by allowing metal termite caps to be placed on the house stumps, or would simply have taken better advantage of prevailing breezes. Some colonists also believed that being high up kept at bay the feverish miasmas which spread low along the ground; certainly it discouraged the entrance of snakes.

Most houses were designed with a simple rectangular plan,

Boodah, designed by Richard Gailey in 1907, show an Indian inspiration and are a case in point. The language of octagonal pavilions is repeated on a grander scale at Cremorne (1905), which was actually designed as a residence for a publican. It is an elaborate timber palace with striking corner pavilions and a large gabled porch. It has a V-shaped plan, with public rooms facing east and private chambers facing west. The whole ensemble is a move towards theatricality and flamboyance reminiscent of the international 'stick style'. However, not all Queensland's timber designers moved in this direction. One of the most influential architects of the period was Robin Dods. Dods trained in Britain in the 1880s and 1890s where he was influenced by C.F.A. Voysey and Norman Shaw, and he later brought an Arts and Crafts approach to the Queensland timber tradition.

His independent thinking was clear from the design of his first houses, which used hardwoods instead of softwoods; rather than paint them white, he oiled and stained them red

in the Scandinavian tradition. His surviving later houses have a far more familiar appearance, using a simple generous plan orientated in the direction of the prevailing north-easterly breezes. In Rangemoor (1910) Dods created an impression of solidity by concealing the house stumps behind timber slats which created a visual 'plinth'. Its façades were sheltered behind deep verandas. These used wide veranda posts and an undulating bressummer in the Federation style to create a fretwork screen below the eaves. Inside, Rangemoor's uncluttered plan encouraged ventilating breezes. The bathrooms were

located between the bedrooms and even included the toilet within the house. Elegant and generous, Dods's timber houses show an original architect who recognized the worth of the domestic timber tradition and was content to work within it.

The finest years of Queenslander construction came to an end at the beginning of World War I. From this point on, houses took on the characteristics of the economical Californian bungalow: shallow pitched gable roofs and bay windows, often with shingle cladding below them. Largely built from builders' merchants' plans, they would remain the standard timber unit

for 25 years after the beginning of the war. It was only after World War II that the hip roof re-emerged, and it did so without the veranda and decoration that had reached their peak in the early years of the century.

ABOVE Ralahyne was extended by Robin Dods in 1904
OVERLEAF The monumental form of Cremorne, 1905, is made up of layers of verandas, both octagonal and rectangular

BEAUDESERT

THE GOTHIC REVIVAL

In England the revival of Gothic architecture entered its most earnest and well-informed phase in the 1830s under the influence of the architect A.W.N. Pugin and his followers. Their views reflected a broader urge among Protestant and Catholic congregations to encourage Christian piety by adopting the practices of the medieval period, then considered to be the great age of faith. Pugin spread his views in his books *Contrasts* (1836) and *The True Principles of Pointed or Christian Gothic Architecture* (1841). These sought to encourage the comprehension of Gothic principles as well as the adoption of Gothic architectural motifs. Pugin believed that one such principle was to ensure honesty of construction by reflecting the means by which a building was erected: 'Construction itself should vary with the material employed, and the designs should be adapted to the material in which they are executed.'

Pugin's views were disseminated right across the British Empire. Here the Gothic Revival's adherents conceded very little to local architectural traditions of the separate countries. Even the independent United States embraced the new style.

The first attempts to translate the Gothic language into Queenland's timber tradition simply achieved a visual resemblance to the Gothic style. Bizarre structures with false towers and false wooden buttresses were built, aping masonry architecture. However, some of the better architects managed to make a more convincing attempt.

G.M.D. Addison was asked to replace a smaller church in an expanding Catholic congregation inland from the Gold Coast. Addison explained his central problem in an interview with the *Beaudesert Despatch* on 9 March 1907. 'The massive picturesque designs of the sacred edifices in older lands have been worked in stone, and the difficulties

LEFT St Mary's church, Beaudesert. The great strength-to-weight ratio of wooden members allows for a very delicate Gothic language

ABOVE The columns with standard capitals are taken straight from the Queenslander house-building tradition

in this new country have been the transference of these designs to wood.'

The Gothic pointed arch was his central problem. Designed to carry the loads of masonry walls, it had no place in a wooden framed building. Addision set about his task by using the great symbol of English medieval carpentry – the hammer-beam roof. This supports a basic V-shaped timber and sheet-metal vault, but the profile of the beams themselves formed a Gothic arch. The central columns that support the vault repeat this shape but their slender size expressed the much lighter loads of a timber structure. Two outer aisles are accommodated in smaller leant-to roofs with separate porches over the various entrances.

An indentation on the outside of the building repeats the Gothic arch, along with a small bell tower and an unusual monogram of the Virgin Mary set into the gable surrounded

LEFT The varied exterior of St Mary's, Beaudesert, seen from the south-west, with Italianate bell tower and Art Nouveau fretwork on the gable end

ABOVE The east end repeats the Gothic arch of the west front, carried through the church by the arch-shape profile of the hammer-beam roof

by fretwork of Art Nouveau inspiration. The whole building is set upon a brick plinth and engenders something of the monumentality Addison was looking for. However, the interior has a delicacy and lightness only possible in wood.

The colonization of Queensland took place during a period in which Australian society was unselfconsciously Anglocentric. This early twentieth-century timber building, built in subtropical Queensland for a largely Irish congregation, was ultimately inspired by the parish churches of medieval England. But because this unlikely mixture is built wholly of Queensland timber, it has a curious visual coherence.

THE FINGER WHARFS

The disadvantage of New South Wales's eucalpyt hardwoods compared to softwoods from overseas was their very hardness as well as their weight. Many were extremely difficult to work and some did not float. As a consequence, they were used only where strength was a prerequisite, such as in wharfs, mineheads, railway sleepers and the like.

The surviving monuments to Australian functional design in timber are the Finger Wharfs in Sydney harbour. The first wharfs appeared in Walsh Bay in the 1830s. Twenty years later these were joined by wharfs in Woolloomooloo Bay. Ship-building facilities grew up swiftly around the bay and by the 1860s Woolloomooloo Bay handled almost half of Sydney's passenger traffic.

In 1900 Sydney suffered an outbreak of bubonic plague carried by rats which had infested the wharfs and quaysides. This led to the formation of the Sydney Harbour Trust, which combated the threat to health by demolishing the old wharfs. Henry Deane Walsh, then engineer-in-chief of the Sydney

Harbour Trust, designed a series of replacements. Pier No. 1 at Walsh Bay was built between 1912 and 1914, followed by Piers 2/3 built between 1916 and 1921. The most imposing structure, however, was that at Woolloomooloo.

This took six years to build, between 1910 and 1916, and remains to this day the largest timber-piled jetty in the world. It sits upon one thousand wooden piles, each the boxed heart of an ironbark trunk. Each pile is 30m (98ft) long and is driven into the soft mud of the harbour. Ironbarks are so heavy that they neither float nor rot in the salty water. The wharf's timber deck is 410m (1,345ft) long and 64m (210ft) wide and upon it sit two timber buildings which run almost the length of the wharf. Originally used to export wool, it has also been used to embark troops and import cars. After a long campaign to save

ABOVE The arched wooden conveyor belt for exporting wool at Woolloomooloo stands behind the dining room of the W Hotel

RIGHT The end of Piers 2/3, Walsh Bay, 1916–21, sits on ironbark piles

ABOVE The central roof-lit corridor between the two buildings on Woolloomooloo wharf, seen from the bar of the W Hotel. Unfortunately the view through to the harbour is blocked by a new development

it, Woolloomooloo wharf was redeveloped in 2000, with mixed results. Now it accommodates the W Hotel and a series of apartments with a disappointing new building at the far end. The bar of the W Hotel shows the monumental room running down between the two buildings that have become one of the world's great covered streets. Fortunately the timber conveyer belts that once transported wool along the wharf to the waiting ships have been retained and restored by the hotel.

It has taken a long time for Sydney's Finger Wharfs to attract the interest they deserve. Even in 1988 the Royal Australian Institute of Architects, when compiling a list of significant

buildings ('444 Sydney Buildings'), drew the wharfs on its map, but made no reference to the buildings themselves. While the city has now come round to appreciating its functional heritage, it did not do so in time to save the wharfs of Darling harbour, and one in Walsh Bay, which have been demolished.

ABOVE The reception area of the W Hotel shows the height of the structure. The uprights remain in Australian eucalpypts but steelwork has been used to reinforce the roof beams. Walls are filled in with closely spaced hardwood studs

OVERLEAF At 410m (1,345ft) long and 64m (210ft) wide, Woolloomooloo wharf is the largest timber piled jetty in the world

LEFT Detail of cross-bracing,
Skyrose Chapel, Whittier,
California, America, by
Jennings & Jones
RIGHT Detail of roof canopy
at Hanover Expo 2000,
Germany, by Thomas Herzog

CHAPTER EIGHT

A FUTURE FOR WOOD

While most of the cities of Western Europe had a substantial proportion of timber buildings, their continous growth eventually militated against the building of further wooden houses. From the sixteenth century, as the population of cities rose, the increasing threat of fire was combated by imposing restrictions upon the number of wooden houses that could be built. The Great Fire of London in 1666 was the most explicit example of the hazard that such dense unplanned wooden cityscapes posed.

The growing scale of cities also encouraged the construction of larger individual buildings to satisfy new functions, particularly in industry and transport. The Industrial Revolution, which originated in Great Britain in the eighteenth century, led to the production of materials like iron, steel and concrete that could span greater distances than wood and enabled the construction of considerably larger buildings.

The development of technically advanced materials found further support at the start of the twentieth century with the standard-bearers of the European Modern Movement in architecture: Gropius, Mies van der Rohe and Le Corbusier. These architects ultimately set the agenda for the rest of the century by proposing to build with an entirely 'contemporary' palette of steel, glass and concrete, more befitting the 'spirit of the age'. Le Corbusier may have been content to build a pine cabin as a present for his wife in 1952, but that is testimony to his asceticism rather than to any fondness for the material. For his clients, he designed almost exclusively in concrete.

The new forms of the International Style also discouraged building in wood on pragmatic as well as ideological grounds. In the United States, Frank Lloyd Wright was sympathetic to the use of wood. His vision of an 'organic architecture' created the possibility of a modernism that employed natural and regional materials. But the oversailing and cantilevered forms he chose required the use of steel and concrete.

Similarly the early Scandinavian modernists Leverentz and

Aalto remained sympathetic to wood, building a number of early works in it but preferring brick and concrete for their major projects. Aalto in particular praised wood for its 'biological characteristics, its limited heat conductivity, its kinship with men and living nature, the pleasant sensation to the touch it gives'. However, he did not design his buildings in wood – he saved the material 'for sensitive architectural details'. For Aalto, wood had psychological benefits, but only as a cladding.

In Russia the revolution of 1917 was based upon an ideology that rejected, wholesale, the cultural products of its own national history. Allied to this was an evident embarrassment that a 'backward' wooden vernacular had not only dominated the countryside but had also made up three-quarters of the buildings in the capital. By the summer of 1919, this discredited wooden legacy had become so worthless that the Moscow City Council officially sanctioned the burning of wooden houses for fuel. By 1920 over 5,000 buildings had been torn down and used as firewood.

Nor did wood have a place in the Bolshevik vision of progress. The 'Rationalist' and 'Constructivist' modernist movements of

LEFT Living room of Hardy House, Bali, Indonesia

ABOVE Belvedere of Mooloomba House, North Stradbroke Island, Queensland, Australia

the 1920s rejected Russia's indigenous wooden tradition. So too did the totalitarian classicism determined by Stalin after he took control of the arts in 1932. After World War II, Russia imposed this prejudice right across Eastern Europe. Wooden houses were replaced in their tens of thousands by concrete mass-housing blocks. At the same time the political elite kept wooden bungalows, or dachas, on the outskirts of Moscow. It was in one of these that Stalin eventually died in 1953.

Both sides in the Cold War shared the same positivist philosophy: that architecture should reflect not regional, climatic or cultural characteristics but an 'international agenda' in keeping with the 'spirit of the age'. Equally they believed the advantages of technology – in every environment and on every scale of project – to be self-evident. Even in the developing countries of the Tropics, where wooden houses are still built in the traditional manner, these traditions have come under threat from the perceived advantages of 'modern' industrial materials. The attractions of a subtle architecture attuned to its native environment have, to a large degree, been overtaken by the attractions of a concrete-block bungalow with air conditioning.

It was not until the 1970s that various energy crises and environmental disasters began to loosen the grip of these certainties. Today raw materials are understood to be finite, and the effects of processing them damaging to the planet. It is now accepted that there is an environmental as well as a financial 'cost' to the manufacture of 'hi-tech' materials such as steel, titanium and aluminium. An unconditional enthusiasm for what Reyner Banham famously described as the 'Machine Age' has been overtaken by anxieties about its long-term environmental consequences.

Wooden architecture continued to be built throughout the twentieth century, albeit outside the gaze of the architectural press. In the US and Scandinavia, wooden-framed houses remained the preferred choice for most house-builders and developers on economic grounds, although technological change affected the timber industry like any other. Laminated boards with superior structural properties to natural timber were developed; the waste products of milling were reworked into inexpensive chipboards.

This has led to a range of modern wooden products. Glue-lamination (Glulam) utilizes layers of wood glued together to produce incredibly light and strong beams. Softwood I-beams have superior strength-to-weight ratios compared to conventional timber beams. Other products encourage a shift away from traditional frames towards an architecture with similarities to log construction, albeit with much thinner walls. Laminated Veneered Lumber (LVL) is a precisely engineered product that effectively peels tree trunks and glues them together to create a product similar to plywood but capable of spanning seven times the distance.

These new wooden materials have created the potential for buildings with broader structural and spatial possibilities than existed in the past. Massive timber members are now a viable structural alternative to steel and concrete, while attitudes to traditional building materials have also changed. It is now widely accepted that contemporary buildings can be considered highly original while also drawing upon such materials to lend a recognizable regional, climatic or cultural character.

ABOVE Thomas Herzog's 16,000sq m (172,000sq ft) timber canopy for Expo 2000 floats 26m (85ft) above the ground in Hanover, Germany
LEFT The potential scale of wooden structures can be seen in the 136m- (446ft-) long Glulam white-pine trusses roofing the departure lounge at Gardermoen Airport, Oslo, Norway, by Nials Torp and Aviaplan

ABOVE Red House, Oslo, Norway, 2002. Open living area, showing its Glulam structure
RIGHT Detail of staircase

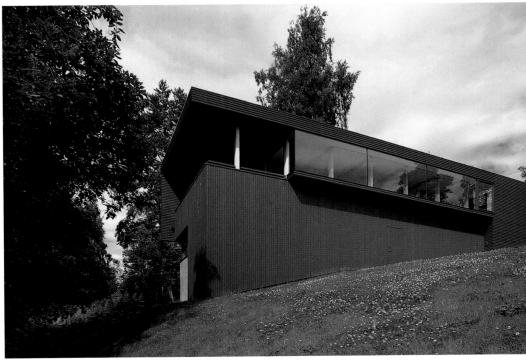

ABOVE Outside terrace with
view north
LEFT Detail of 'skirt-and-blouse'
tradition of cladding, with
vertical and horizontal members

WOOD AND ITS CONTEXT

In 2002 the young Norwegian architects Einar Jarmund and Hakon Vigsnæs designed a new house in Oslo whose striking new form used a similar palette of wooden elements to its more traditional neighbours. The Red House is set on a steeply sloping site in a forested western suburb of the city. It is clad in weatherboards which change direction from vertical on the lower floor to horizontal on the upper in recognition of the 1930s 'skirt and blouse' tradition of Norwegian architecture.

The long rectangular plan projects at right angles to the slope in order to open up broad views while minimizing its impact upon the views enjoyed by houses further up the hill.

The layouts of the two floors are determined by the needs of the different generations living there. The entrance level is explicitly designed for the use of the parents. It has a bedroom, kitchen and open area for the entertainment of guests, ending in an open terrace overlooking the landscape to the south.

The lower storey, partly set into the hillside, accommodates the children's bedrooms and a soundproofed den with views through the slit windows towards the north-east. This gives the house a chunky S-shaped façade when viewed from the valley. It is framed in glue-laminated timber made from Norwegian spruce in 10x20cm (4x8in) vertical and 10x30cm (4x12in) horizontal members. Its vibrant colour reflects the local habit of painting wooden houses, albeit wryly – as the choice is said to reflect the client's temperament. All the constituent elements of the Red House tailor it to fit neatly into a sensitive vernacular context, but its individuality remains unsuppressed.

The Swiss architect Peter Zumthor has also recognized the potential of wood to engender a sense of belonging within a sympathetic context, but in surroundings that are rural rather than suburban. He was commissioned to build a tiny country chapel at St Benedict in Zumvig, high up in the mountain passes of Switzerland. Following traditional Alpine practice, he built it in wood but the building does not ape the Swiss vernacular. On the contrary, its footprint is elliptical, with one rounded corner that oversails the steep valley. The building's skin is clad in shingles whose colours change with their orientation – grey to the north and dark brown to the south. The entrance-way is asymmetrically slotted into the uphill corner, the door fitting between the framework of interior studs that stand apart from the chapel's curving walls. The simple, curving interior channels attention towards the altar lit by a continuous clerestory window. The building deliberately invokes a vernacular

tradition while in no way resembling a historic building. It complements the striking landscape in stark contrast to the new concrete block houses scattered further down the valley. At the same time the logic of its form and construction is entirely contemporary.

This sense of belonging is, of course, relative to the context of the building, which is often less than idyllic. Japan has as extensive a tradition of domestic wooden architecture as any country in the world, but its urban topography has now changed beyond recognition. When in 2002 Tatsuo Kawanishi

**ABOVE LEFT The Red House.
Outside terrace with view north**

ABOVE Jarmund and Vigsnæs's
design affords views deep into
the forest on the other side of
the valley

Architects ignored the prevailing concrete orthodoxy of post-war Japan and built a clinic and pharmacy building it implemented the minimalist agenda of many contemporary Japanese architects, but did so in wood. Even in Kyoto the use of this most Japanese of materials now looks bizarre and daring amid all the concrete and power lines. Here, the use of wood provides an impression of warmth and approachability despite the building's pure modernist lines, which suits its purpose as a community building perfectly.

LEFT St Benedict's chapel, Zumvig, Switzerland, by Peter Zumthor
ABOVE The elliptical form of St Benedict's is entered asymmetrically

ABOVE & TOP Tatsuo Kawanishi Architects' clinic and pharmacy building is set in a typical suburb of Kyoto, Japan

WOOD AND NATURE

A number of contemporary architects now use wood in response to the wider needs of the environment, viewing the site as a microcosm of the planet. Several Australian architects, in response to the specific climate and building traditions of the Pacific Rim, have consciously rejected the early colonial habit of swift construction in softwoods, and have chosen instead to build with the magnificent Australian hardwoods.

Richard Leplastrier has built a number of private houses that reveal a very studied approach to the site. His Forest House on Queensland's Sunshine Coast is located in one of the richest natural habitats in Australia, where the tropical trees of Queensland meet the temperate hardwoods of New South Wales. When he was commissioned his clients were already camped on their site: a forest clearing. Leplastrier chose simply to formalize their existing way of living. The couple's

two small huts were replaced by a raised platform supporting two pavilions that echo their original orientation.

Leplastrier has worked and studied in Japan, and shares the Japanese sense of responsibility for the use of a felled tree. When the clearing was widened to accommodate the new building the trees that were cut down were incorporated into the design. All additional supplies were sourced from recycled timber. As a result, the house is built in a medley of different Australian hardwoods. The supporting structure was built from the ultra-strong eucalypt ironbark. This came from

Gympie in Queensland and the 30cm (12in) diameter posts are simply buried in the ground. Aware that after 70 or 80 years it would require splinting and re-footing, Leplastrier left instructions. The platform itself is built in the native Queensland eucalypt spotted gum. The structure of the pavilion is blackbutt and the walls and joinery of the first pavilion are from rosewood – part of the excess timber used in the renovation of Parliament House. Window frames are of yellow stringy-bark, the doors and joinery Queensland maple.

Leplastrier believes in constructing buildings in such a way

that they can easily be taken down and moved, or disassembled so that their members can be re-employed elsewhere. With the help of builder Brian Paylor and wood craftsman Philip Green, he made a range of elegant wood joints to achieve this aim.

The shape of the house responds to the practical demands of the rainforest site. The whole structure has been lifted on a platform to avoid the waterlogged forest floor and Queensland snakes. This provides high-level views into the forest and allows easier access to sunlight, which provides power through the solar panels on the roof. The garage has been constructed

ABOVE Forest House, Queensland, Australia. The bathroom and tai-chi room are located in a second, smaller pavilion. The whole building sits upon a hardwood raft above the forest floor
TOP LEFT Kitchen window
BOTTOM LEFT The study of Forest House looks out into the rainforest

ABOVE Mooloomba House, North
Stradbroke Island, Australia.
Belvedere
RIGHT View into the main pavilion
BELOW The panel module is based
on the size of plywood sheets

as a separate pavilion uphill, with a long curved walkway connecting it to the house and avoiding the need to climb upstairs to the platform. The first pavilion houses the main bedroom, study, dining room and kitchen in an open plan. The second pavilion accommodates the bathroom and guest bedroom/tai-chi room.

Inspired by the economy and beauty of wooden boats, Leplastrier's house is designed as a raft for forest living. But he views its constituent members as objects he has borrowed which have the potential for another life beyond the building itself.

A similarly eloquent case for the use of Australian hardwoods can be found in the work of Brisbane practice Andresen O'Gorman. Mooloomba House, built as a weekend house for the architects, lies on a ridge overlooking the sea on North Stradbroke Island off the southern Queensland coast. Its structure is designed in the eucalypt spotted gum, an intensely strong wood which is, however, notoriously difficult to work. When timber dries its moisture content drops to about 10–15 per cent, in equilibrium with the moisture content of its surroundings. When the wood dries below the fibre saturation

point (a moisture content of about 30 per cent), it shrinks. Moreover, it does not shrink equally in both directions. Hardwoods typically shrink between 3 and 6 per cent radially but twice that amount in the plane of its length. This can result in warping, checking, cracking and twisting, often a source of charm in, for instance, old oak buildings, but in some of the eucalypts the effect can render the timber unusable.

Peter O'Gorman discovered that if you split a green spotted gum member in two and then turn one half upside down and bolt it back to itself, the forces can be made to act against one another, in equilibrium. The straightness of Mooloomba's composite members testifies to the success of this method. The wood's strength accounts for this slim diameter, which allowed the architects to explore a visual language of screens and lattices rather than heavy frames.

Mooloomba is made up of two parallel linear structures facing north–south. To the east the composite columns are laid out on a 1,200m (4,000ft) grid determined by the standard size of plywood sheets. This structure supports a first-floor study and sleeping cubicles and a long narrow corridor leading to a final belvedere with views over the sea. It sits on 'Queenslander-

type' stumps across the Stradbroke undergrowth, forming a delicately proportional screen based on the Fibonacci series.

To the west are three separate chambers constructed in a far more rustic interpretation of a wooden house. Here, whole cypress trunks are sunk deep into the sand to support rough-sawn hardwood rafters with an irregular spacing. This being an entirely sand island, the water drains away very quickly and all the vertical columns remain free from rot. Within the house these trunks are stripped of bark, but outside the bark is left. The timberwork seems less ordered, almost random, as if responding to the wooded landscape around.

Mooloomba's use of wood follows a determination to make the minimal intervention in the landscape, in stark contrast to the masonry bungalows of modern Queensland. This principle can be seen most explicitly in the design of Rosebery House in the Highgate Hill suburb of Brisbane. Here, the house is approached along a standard suburban street but is found occupying a remnant of bushland left over after the area's development. Like Mooloomba House, the design of Rosebery House resists the temptation to build across the slope in pursuit of the best range of views, but instead reinforces the space of the gully in which it sits. It sinks into the landscape, presenting

a woven layered façade behind which the form of the house remains inscrutable. And, as at Mooloomba, the garden feels like a temporary borrowing of the natural topography rather than its permanent partition and destruction.

Brit Andresen denies any conscious influence from Japanese architecture. The major timbers are stained black with a pigmented oil-based solution to give these slender members visual weight, not to invoke a Japanese duotone palette. However, the thoughtful integration of structures with the natural world betrays a sensibility reminiscent of traditional Japanese design.

ABOVE The Hardy House, near
Ubud, Bali. Bedroom
ABOVE RIGHT Bathroom of
the Guest Pavilion
BELOW The curving entrance
corridor has adobe walls and a
bamboo roof
FAR RIGHT The living area sits
above a pond on a platform

A more playful, if less rigorous, approach to the integration of a wooden house into its habitat can be seen near Ubud in Bali. The Hardy House, by C.Y. Kuan, uses wood both for its environmental qualities and also to create a rather theatrical effect.

The house is entered via a long dark curved passageway designed to keep out Balinese spirits who can only travel in straight lines. Inside, three buildings are set within a garden compound in accordance with Balinese practice. A separate service building and a guest pavilion complement the main house.

The house straddles a pool of water and is approached by a bamboo bridge. It is raised on a post-and-truss frame constructed from recycled 8m (26ft) long telegraph poles in ironwood, which, as the name suggests, is an exceptionally durable hardwood. This frame is then cross-braced by whole unworked tree trunks. The inspiration for the use of the latter came accidentally when the model for the project required last-minute struts for reinforcement. Twigs from the lawn were used, and their rustic effect was enjoyed enough to warrant full-scale inclusion in the finished house. Branches of sono wood were gathered from the roadside in neighbouring Java.

The floors and walls are made of the native Indonesian hardwood merbau. This came in very large slabs up to 1m (3ft) wide and 3m (10ft) long, which were deliberately abutted in an ad hoc manner to form the ground-floor platform, which is attached to the frame by wooden pegs. The edge of this platform is left with an irregular profile of slabs and beams oversailing the water. Throughout, the building rejoices in this over-engineered 'imprecision'.

The enclosed upper storey maximizes views over a valley of paddy fields. Below, the ground floor is left completely open, apart from the glazed cubes at either end, which contain a kitchen and study. The open social space in between acts as a natural living room, framing a view of the landscape beyond.

The guest pavilion has an ironwood structure, with smaller perimeter posts made from old clove trees. The rafters are also made from clove trees, and the roof is thatched. Walls, panel and floors are merbau planks. The pavilion encloses an internal space for sleeping and shields an outside bathroom from the view of the house. Like the central living space, this provides as simple a statement as possible of an architecture that solely seeks to augment the pleasures of the landscape.

ORGANIC WOOD

E. Fay Jones was an American architect and acolyte of Frank Lloyd Wright. His work consistently upheld and developed Wright's 'organic architecture', a design ideal that sought to integrate a building style with the needs of its inhabitants and the existing character of the surrounding landscape.

In partnership with Maurice Jennings, Jones built a series of wooden chapels, the largest of which is Skyrose Chapel in Whittier, California. This was commissioned by a large crematorium, Rose Hills, in the suburbs of Los Angeles (a setting reminiscent of Evelyn Waugh's satirical Whispering Glades in *The Loved One*). Jennings & Jones brought gravitas to their church designs through the use of an all-wooden palette, in this case spruce. While the ecclesiastical nature of the project did not originally determine the choice of this material, over time wood became a defining characteristic of the office's religious work.

Skyrose Chapel is roughly triangular in profile, with a wide central nave flanked by two side aisles lit from above by a central section of glass roof. The eastern end is similarly covered by a huge glass wall which allows caskets to be placed in front of both the altar and a huge vista of Los Angeles.

On either side of the nave massive wooden columns rise up to the ceiling, while the cross-braces between them are built on a much smaller scale. Here Jones developed a system he called the 'operative opposite' which was inspired by the masonry flying buttresses that support the walls of Gothic cathedrals. These balance the outward thrust of the walls by bracing them with external supports. Because wooden trusses hold members in tension as well as compression, Jones could use cross-braces to bind the structure together from the inside – hence, they represent the 'operative opposite' of the buttress. This is, of course, true of many wooden buildings that use tie

ABOVE Skyrose Chapel, Whittier, California, USA, hugs the ground with its wide low roof. The cross-bracing of the interior is continued onto the west front
LEFT The vault
FAR LEFT North side aisle

ABOVE Steel beams are set
across the shingle surface of
the Price Residence, Corona del
Mar, California, but the
structure is wooden

RIGHT Central courtyard of
the Price Residence. The
staircase leads to the
entertainment pod

beams to carry load, but the work of Jones & Jennings is distinct because it elaborates these trusses into the central gesture of their design. A 26m (85ft) vault leads the eye up into a mass of intermingling cross-braces like a forest canopy. These are joined together by steel connectors which have a hollow core, leaving a void running down the centre line of the vault.

Through this latticework of thin wooden members, the whole composition is meticulously orchestrated to create a highly symmetrical impression. In this regard Skyrose Chapel is only partly reminiscent of 'organic architecture' as conceived by Wright or the Greenes because, though organic in material, it is also monumental in form. Such monumentality, however, is tempered during the day by the motion of the Californian sun, which creates shifting patterns of light and shadow that overlay a visual asymmetry upon the nave.

An entirely alternative 'organicism' is achieved by the Price Residence in Corona del Mar, California, a truly bizarre and original work in wood designed for one of the most remarkable architectural clients of the twentieth century. Joe Price first became involved in commissioning buildings when he convinced his father to employ Frank Lloyd Wright to build what was to become the famous Price Tower in Bartlesville, Oklahoma. Wright went on to design houses for the Price family in Bartlesville and Phoenix, Arizona. When it came to his own house in Bartlesville, however, Price chose Wright's pupil the maverick architect Bruce Goff. After Goff's death, Price moved to California, where he commissioned another design in the same style from Goff's acolyte Bart Prince.

The Price Residence occupies what appears to be a nondescript site in a suburban cul-de-sac, but in fact backs onto cliffs in a spectacular setting overlooking the Pacific. Here practically nothing is standard, and every element is bespoke. It took a

single craftsman two years to place the shingles across its undulating form, which curves around a central courtyard swimming pool. Within it a sequence of spaces lead away from the street, each assigned an increasing degree of privacy.

Beyond the driveway, the front door is approached by a series of stairs which curve both around and into a cocooning form. At the top of this lies Joe Price's office, itself a remarkable ensemble of wooden elements. The walls and ceiling are made from layers of clear vertical-grain Oregon fir which protrude from the walls and ceiling in a series of arches. The curvaceous desk and matching wastepaper basket are made of Finnish birch plywood. The office chair is solid maple burr.

From behind this desk the occupant of the office can open a hidden door and invite visitors into his entertainment room and bar area, suspended over the swimming pool in a series of three interconnected wooden 'pods'. These pods are supported by composite columns consisting of a series of glue-laminated beams of Oregon fir that fan out in a circle around a hidden air duct. The column members are wood but have stainless-steel

joints whose hinges are hidden by wooden dowels. The thin copper fin that runs the length of the member maintains the notion of the wood sandwiching the metal, but this is not structurally the case, as the fin only sits in a 0.6cm (¼in) groove. It is simply a wooden frame with metal joints. In this case timber was chosen as much for reasons of safety as aesthetics. Corona del Mar sits firmly within the Californian fault zone, and Prince favoured a wooden structure not only to create the shape he wanted but also to respond to the threat of earthquakes. In addition, the roof was designed out of airtight solid laminated wooden members to counteract the danger of fire. This acts as a heavy wooden 'plate' over the entire house. The choice of wood also allows the structure to form the surfaces of an extraordinary interior. Where the pods interconnect, their sides are left open and the structural members are left as a skeleton of arches.

Finally the chosen few may be invited through a door hidden in the reception-room floor. This leads down a circular spiral staircase, which curls within the composite column of a pod to the pool below. Around the pool are wrapped the dining

ABOVE LEFT The Price Residence entrance stairway is wrapped within a cocooning structure
ABOVE RIGHT The dining/living room overlooks the pool
LEFT View across the interior of the first-floor pods

ABOVE Tea-house designed by
Kisho Kurakawa on the lower-
ground floor of Price Residence

LEFT Detail of stairs on the
front terrace
RIGHT Mr Price's office

room, kitchen and entertainment area. These rooms are shaped
by the underside of the pods, which stand like huge umbrellas,
the gaps between them creating skylights. The last and most
intimate space is hidden behind a concealed door leading to
the floor below, further down the slope, where Prince designed
a gallery looking out to sea. Next to the gallery, the Japanese
architect Kisho Kurakawa designed a tea-house for Joe Price
and Japanese craftsmen were sent over to build it. The tea-
house allows its guests to take tea surrounded by Japanese
furnishings while overlooking the Californian coast.

'Organic architect' is a title Bart Prince has consciously
rejected whereas Fay Jones wore it as a badge of honour. What
is certain is that a number of American architects have inherited
from Wright the determination to make architecture that is
both modernist and highly individualistic. In this they have
been inspired both by the beauty of the American landscape
and by the expressive potential of natural materials, particularly
timber – a combination that has resulted in some highly imag-
inative and unmistakably American wooden architecture.

HI-TECH VERNACULAR

The final part of French president François Mitterrand's Grand Project opened in 1998, thousands of miles from Paris in New Caledonia, a French dependency in the South Pacific 1,450km (900 miles) east of Australia. The Jean-Marie Tjibaou Cultural Centre in Noumea, dedicated to the life and art of the island's Kanak population, was conceived to placate the ethnic Kanak majority. It is a cultural centre dedicated to the leader of the Kanak independence movement, Jean-Marie Tjibaou, tragically murdered by one of his own supporters in 1989. Interestingly the emblem Kanak nationalists chose when they emerged during the 1970s was that of the local wooden village house, particularly the *morara* or 'chief's house' – a symbol of community identity.

Renzo Piano, the Italian architect famous for his joint authorship of the hi-tech Pompidou Centre in Paris, won the open competition for its design. Piano's scheme is distinguished by his use of a series of forms explicitly derived from the vernacular wooden tradition of the Kanaks.

TOP The Jean-Marie Tjibaou Cultural Centre, Noumea, New Caledonia, 1998, is orientated to face the prevailing breezes across Magenta Bay
LEFT Detail of 'case'

ABOVE Roof structure of traditional Kanak hut

Traditional Kanak culture has no written system; they are a people without a documented history. Instead, they have developed a mythological system which Piano, in collaboration with anthropologist Alban Bensa, incorporated into the plan. The centre's design is based on a Kanak ceremonial path that would traditionally have been lined with trees and culminated in the chief's hut. Piano has substituted the exhibition and seminar rooms for the 'trees', here accommodated in structures he calls 'cases' which make up the 'village' of the complex. Traditional Kanak huts are simple bound post-and-beam structures with conical roofs that draw off the heat of the day into the high ceiling voids. This climatic tradition is translated into Piano's 'cases'. In their design and orientation Piano emulates the Kanak principles of passive ventilation, but in a highly technological form. The cases are positioned in response to the strong prevailing Pacific Trade Winds that cross the site from the ocean, periodically at cyclonic velocities.

Tropical iroko timbers were laminated into curved members up to 28m (92ft) high, which are interlaced at the bottom with horizontal curved slats and left open at the top to create a comb-like shape. Behind them sits a secondary skin of glass and steel louvres. The design of the façade included computer simulation and wind-tunnel testing to create a system that responds automatically to the intensity of the breeze, opening and closing louvres to ventilate the building passively.

Piano has reinterpreted the Kanak architectural tradition with imported and engineered wood and sophisticated technology. The result is a highly original new building which attempts to represent Kanak culture through its age-old and symbiotic relationship with the natural world. The Jean-Marie Tjibaou Cultural Centre thus avoids reworking a specific vernacular and stands as its own powerful symbol of wooden architecture's harmonious relationship with nature.

ABOVE The 'cases' each accommodate a gallery accessed by a conventional one-storey structure behind

LEFT Two separate latticeworks of iroko timber members surround each 'case'
RIGHT The iroko timber has turned silver from the saline winds coming from Magenta Bay

INNOVATION IN WOOD

The Downland Gridshell was built in 2002 to provide the Weald and Downland Open-Air Museum with an exhibition space and workshop where historic timber-framed buildings could be publicly restored. The architects Edward Cullinan and timber engineers the Green Oak Company used traditional green oak to create a complex structure that could not have existed without the technological innovations of the last hundred years.

Gridshells are formed by laying out flat long pliable strips of wood, which are then curved in two dimensions and attached to each other to form a naturally occurring curved shape. While simple gridshells have been used in vernacular architecture in Africa and South America for hundreds of years, it was the design of car bodies and aircraft fuselages in the last century that opened up the possibility of using them to tackle more ambitious spans. In the 1970s, Frei Otto in Germany designed a series of experimental structures that made very large spans possible and the sophisticated curvilinear form at Downland extends their capabilities further.

Oak was chosen to make the laths for a variety of reasons. It is durable and does not require surface treatment. It is also stronger, allowing for the smallest cross sections to be used. In addition, it is stiffer than other woods but it also has a higher bending strength so it can reach a tighter radius before failing. Finally, it can also be used 'green', for the high moisture content of the timber allows it to be formed into the necessary curves and then locked into shape. Once in place the timber can be allowed to dry naturally, strengthening the structure.

The timber used was not English but French, as it was calculated that it would cost the environment less to import sustainable timber from France than from the north of England. Oak trees, once 'the Sussex weed', could not be supplied locally. As oak does not grow to the required lengths without becoming too dense to bend into shape, individual 6m (20ft) lengths were instead scarf-jointed together to form 35m (115ft) strips. These strips were double-layered into the structural laths. In preparation, a basement level had been cut into the hillside and its walls supported glue-laminated beams and a solid timber floor. This was cut to the serpentine perimeter of the projected gridshell and would act as a template on which the ends of the laths would rest. Above this a scaffolding platform was erected at the projected height of the 'valleys' of the shell. The laths were laid out diagonally across the linear plan of the structure in two opposing directions.

As the laths slowly assumed their shape they moved across each other, connected by clamps that held one lath tight while allowing the other to move. The layers were also held apart by sheer blocks to ensure that they would act correctly as a composite member. Computer-modelling ascertained that in the 'valleys' of the undulating structure stresses would be greater and here laths needed to be placed at 50cm (20in) centres. Climbing over the 'hills', they could afford to fan out to 1m (40in) apart.

Once formed, the structure was 50m (164ft) long. Its width varies from 11 to 16m (36–52ft) wide and it stands 10m (33ft) high on the 'hills', 7m (23ft) in the 'valleys'. The whole structure was clad in red cedar panels faceted across the surface.

ABOVE Downland Gridshell, Weald and Downland Open-Air Museum, England, 2002. The entrance allows forklifts to bring in sections of historic timber buildings
LEFT Red cedar panels articulate the curves of the Downland Gridshell
OVERLEAF The Gridshell's interior

LEFT Eaves detail from
Nishi-Hongan-ji, Kyoto, Japan
RIGHT Shingling
reinterpreted by Bart Prince
in the Price Residence,
Corona-del-Mar,
California, USA

CONCLUSION

A DIFFERENT APPROACH

Viewed from a contemporary perspective, where the built environment is dominated by concrete, masonry and steel, historic wooden buildings appear almost absurdly fragile. This lends the survivors a particular pathos, such as the few remaining stave churches that continue to evoke the last flowering of Christian-Nordic art before the cataclysm of the Black Death. But this impression of fragility is partly misleading. The Buddhist Japanese, who believed in the transitory nature of all things, built wooden architecture that has survived for over 1,300 years. They knew that to build with wood required a complete understanding of its natural characteristics, but that if they applied that knowledge, their buildings could stand indefinitely. The delicate Phoenix Hall at Uji, for example, has survived from the eleventh century because the carpenters knew to set the building on stone footings, to protect the end-grain of the wood at all times and to add regular ventilation slots to allow the structure to dry out quickly. Japanese carpenters even used trees from the northern slopes of mountains to construct the northern façades of buildings, knowing that the tree had already addressed the demands of that orientation during the course of its life. Thus, the survival of historic wooden buildings is often a consequence of their not being actively destroyed rather than of any inherent limitations in the material.

The longevity of Japanese wooden architecture is also testimony to the respect Japanese carpenters had for individual trees, believing that each possessed a spirit whose wasteful exploitation would have spiritual repercussions. Japanese rules of carpentry therefore prized thrift as greatly as precision. In Western Europe, by contrast, 70 per cent of forests were destroyed during the course of the Middle Ages as rapidly expanding populations encroached on them in search of arable land and burnt the trees as fuel. It was the Western European approach that was adopted worldwide, and to this day major forests around the world are under severe threat from both legal and illegal

TOP The Kizhi Pogost remains a powerful symbol of the Russian tradition of wooden architecture

ABOVE The Phoenix Hall, Uji, Japan, whose construction, prepared for the end of the world, has survived for nearly 900 years

clearance. The vast majority of this destruction serves to satisfy an immediate demand for land, not for the trees that stand on it. Central to the problem is the inability of governments to see long-term economic value in forestry. However, today, in Europe at least, a different view prevails and European forests are once again growing. The total forest cover has grown by 30 per cent since 1999 and each year it swells by an area the size of Cyprus. The vast majority is planted to provide sustainable forestry where timber is selectively harvested while increasing the forest mass. This provides an economic yield from the trees without destroying the forest.

Unfortunately some of our central ideals of what constitutes 'architecture' oppose the practice of building in wood. These are the ideals of monumentality and permanence that are inspired by stone buildings such as Greek temples, Gothic cathedrals, Islamic mosques and the like. In reality, the seemingly permanent monuments of today – skyscrapers, airports and factories – are nothing of the sort. The average skyscraper, for instance, will require a major overhaul or replacement after only 30 or 40 years, and steel frames will last at best 150 years, whereas oak frames survive for over 800. But the sheer mass of these structures gives them the appearance of permanence, an illusion that comes at a tremendous cost to the environment. Each year buildings account for half of the raw materials consumed around the world, and 45 per cent of annual energy consumption is used for the heating, lighting and ventilation of these spaces. Their environmental impact could be reduced by a more careful choice of materials. 'Embodied energy', for example, is an assessment of the amount of energy required to extract a raw material from nature and process it into a finished building product. It takes only 1.5 mJ/kg to convert wood into the building material timber, compared to 35 mJ/kg for steel and 435 mJ/kg for aluminium. Moreover, the processing of these costly

materials greatly increases global warming by releasing CO_2 into the atmosphere. Wood, however, acts as a carbon sink, holding CO_2 out of the atmosphere and lessening its effect. In addition, timber has excellent natural thermal insulatory properties, which means that timber houses use far less energy during the course of their lifetime than those made of masonry, concrete or steel.

Using wood from sustainable sources will only ever constitute part of an environmental strategy, but the attributes of this, our first building material, might encourage an alternative approach to the built environment. Such an approach would regard the act of building not as one of permanent change but of temporary rearrangement, whose forms should retain the possibility of being moved, reconfigured or entirely recycled. While wooden buildings can last for thousands of years, they are also entirely biological, non-toxic and ultimately biodegradable. In the face of growing environmental threats, building with wood may prove not only desirable but necessary.

ABOVE The Nanzenin sub-temple of Nanzen-ji. Kyoto, illustrates the continuous Japanese interest in the gentle integration of architecture with nature
LEFT The bell tower of Petajavesi, Finland, is the work of the church designer's grandson
OVERLEAF Downland Gridshell, England, by Edward Cullinan Architects, 2002

ARCADE PLATE A horizontal beam that runs along a line of arcade posts in an aisled building supporting the common rafters.

BALLOON FRAME A technique of framing first made possible by the industrial production of metal nails during the 19th century which allowed smaller members to be nailed together into a sturdy but very lightweight frame. In balloon framing, the studs (vertical members) extend the full height of the building, from foundation plate to rafter plate.

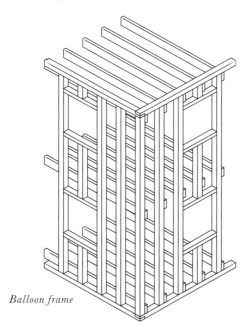

Balloon frame

BARGE The overhanging end of a gabled roof.

BARGE-BOARD A wooden board, fixed to the lower edge of a barge solely to hide the ends of horizontal roof timbers. Often used to display carved decoration.

BLOCKWORK Also called horizontal log construction. In this technique of wooden

Blockwork

construction tree trunks are laid horizontally on top of each other to create walls.

BOXED HEART The squared centre of a tree trunk. Before the end of the 18th century these would be hewn by hand using an axe or adze.

BRACE A secondary member of a timber frame that strengthens the right angle between two main members.

passing brace A member run diagonally across several horizontal and vertical members in order to strengthen them against sideways movement.

scissor brace Used in pairs to cross diagonally between rafters to triangulate them into a form of truss.

BRACKET A short timber member that projects from one member to support another.

Bracket

BRACKET SET (CHINESE) A system of cantilevered layers of mortice-and-tenon joints used in Far Eastern carpentry to distribute the very heavy loads of the roof. This specific bracket set is a *zhuanjiao puzuo*, or 'a bracket set on a column at the corner of a building'.

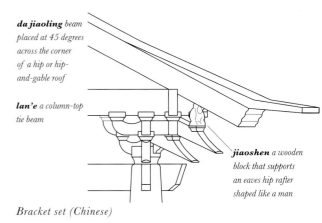

da jiaoling *beam placed at 45 degrees across the corner of a hip or hip-and-gable roof*

lan'e *a column-top tie beam*

jiaoshen *a wooden block that supports an eaves hip rafter shaped like a man*

Bracket set (Chinese)

BRACKET SET (JAPANESE) A system of brackets connected by mortice-and-tenon joints used in Far Eastern carpentry to distribute the very heavy loads of the roof. This particular corner set comes from the Eastern Pagoda, Yukushi-ji.

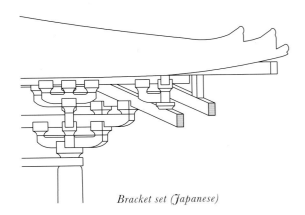

Bracket set (Japanese)

BRESSUMMER The sill beam of an upper wall that runs on beyond the wall to support a jetty.

flying bressummer A horizontal timber carrying deeply projecting eaves.

CARPENTER GOTHIC A style of mid-19th-century US domestic wooden architecture that used an eclectic mixture of superficially Gothic motifs produced by the fretsaw.

CLAPBOARDING Horizontal boards overlapped to provide an external wall covering; can be used either horizontally or vertically. The name derives from the practice of coopers who used clapboards to make barrels. (USA; WEATHERBOARDING in Europe.)

COLLAR A horizontal roof member which spans between the rafters.

CONSOLE A form of carved ornamental bracket that features paired volutes resembling a classical carved masonry console.

Console

END GIRT A horizontal beam within a timber wall which runs halfway between and parallel to the groundsill and top-plate. Used to stiffen structure.

ENGINEERED TIMBER The generic term used to describe a wide range of wood-based products that combine wood or wood fibre with other substances, usually adhesives. They have been altered for a combination of three reasons – for greater technical performance, to create greater homogeneity and in order to utilize offcuts of the timber industry which would otherwise go to waste.

GROUNDSILL The first horizontal timber laid to construct a wooden building. Often placed on a stone footing but sometimes placed directly onto the ground.

GAMBREL ROOF Distinctive dual-angle profile supposedly derived from the shape of a horse's back leg (originally European).

GLULAM A modern timber product where layers of wood are laminated together by glue producing a stronger cross section than natural wood.

HALF-TIMBERED Refers to a framed construction whose members are left visible on the outside of the building. The name is reputed to be derived from the practice of halving logs before use.

HIPPED ROOF A roof made up of four pitches.

JETTY An upper wall cantilevered beyond a lower one.

GLOSSARY

JOINTS The junctions between wooden members.

butt joint The simplest form of joint where the end of one piece of timber touches another.

lap joint A joint formed by simply overlapping two thinned-down members, which are then hammered through with a wooden dowel (a form of nail) to secure the joint.

scarf joint A number of laps are used to join two pieces of timber together in a line.

mortice-and-tenon joint

A mortice is a hole cut in a wooden member in order to receive a tenon, part of another member cut specifically to fit it.

Butt joint

Lap joint

Scarf joint

Scarf joint

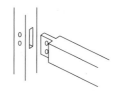

Mortice-and-tenon joint

LATH A thin narrow flat strip of wood used to provide a key for plaster.

LAMINATED VENEERED LUMBER (LVL) A precisely engineered product that effectively peels tree trunks and glues them together producing a product similar to plywood but capable of spanning seven times the distance of ply.

MORTICE-AND-TENON JOINT See JOINTS.

NOGGING Brickwork used as an infilling in a half-timbered building.

PLATE The horizontal member that runs along the top or bottom of a timber frame.

PENDANT A short piece of timber suspended from above, often from a jetty, with a decorative carved lower end.

PLATFORM FRAME A system of framing that, like balloon framing, was pioneered in the nineteenth century with the mass production of metal nails. However, here each floor is framed separately. Floor joists are laid on each top plate and these in turn support another sill from which studs rise to another top plate.

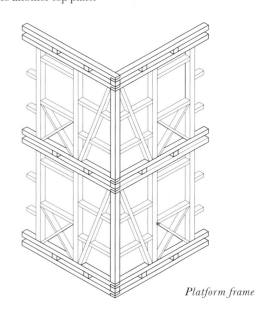

Platform frame

PLYWOOD A wooden board made from sheets of wood glued together with their grains running at right angles to each other.

PURLIN A longitudinal supporting member that runs perpendicular to the slope of the roof.

RAFTER Supporting members that run parallel to the slope of the roof.

RATTAN A solid timber vine that grows in the jungles of Indonesia; often used as a means of securing wooden frames or roofing materials.

ROOFS Hip, gable, hip-and-gable, and gambrel.

Hip roof *Gable roof*

Hip-and-gable roof *Gambrel roof*

SHINGLES Thin slices of wood used to cover walls and roofs.

SHINGLE STYLE A style that flourished in the US between 1879 and 1900 in which the walls and roofs of wooden buildings were covered with shingles.

SPROCKET Small timber angle which projects from the bottom of common rafters beyond the top of the wall to provide protecting eaves.

STICK STYLE A term coined by the architectural historian Vincent Scully in his writings in the 1950s to refer to American buildings of 1860–90 which had a number of stick-like features of applied ornamantation influenced by the Gothic Revival, the English half-timbered cottage, Swiss chalets and even Russian dachas.

Sprocket

STUD A vertical timber member serving within the wall of a timber frame.

TIMBER A building material produced by the felling and working of tree trunks and branches.

TRUSS A triangulated frame made from several pieces of timber jointed together which maintains its shape under load.

crown post truss A central support in a truss which runs from the middle of a tie beam up to a collar purlin.

Crown post truss

king post truss A central support in a truss which runs from the middle of a tie beam up to the ridge beam.

King post truss

queen post truss Pairs of posts that act as compression members within a roof truss. They sit between a tie beam and a collar.

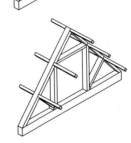

Queen post truss

WATTLE AND DAUB A material used to infill the panels created in half-timbered buildings. Consists of 'wattle', small strips of wood woven to create a latticework mesh, and 'daub', a mixture of clay, chopped straw and animal dung. Often covered with limewash.

WEATHERBOARDING Horizontal boards overlapped to provide an external wall covering; can be used either horizontally or vertically. (Europe; CLAPBOARDING in North America.)

BIBLIOGRAPHY

THE FAR EAST

Azby Brown, S., *The Genius of Japanese Carpentry* (Tokyo 1989)

Boyd, Andrew, *Chinese Architecture and Town Planning* (University of Chicago Press 1962)

Carver, N.F., *Form & Space in Japanese Architecture* (Documan Press 1993)

Chan, Charis, *Imperial China* (Penguin 1992)

Cheng, Qinhua, ed., *Tales of the Forbidden City* (Foreign Languages Press, Beijing 1997)

Coaldrake, W.H., *The Way of the Carpenter* (Tokyo 1990)

Coaldrake, W.H., *Architecture and Authority in Japan* (Routledge, London 1996)

Durston, Diane, *Old Kyoto* (Kodansha America 1986)

Guo, Qinghua, *The Structure of Chinese Timber Architecture* (1999)

Hirai, Kiyoshi, *Feudal Architecture of Japan* (Tokyo 1980)

Kirby, John B., *From Castle to Teahouse: Japanese Architecture of the Momoyama Period* (1962)

Liu, Guanghua, *Beijing: The Cornucopia of Classical Chinese Architecture* (Singapore 1982)

Liu, Guanghua, *Chinese Architecture* (London 1989)

Mosher, Gouverneur, *Kyoto: A Contemplative Guide* (1964)

Nakashima, Ryan, 'Escape from the Concrete Jungle', *Bangkok Post*, 20 May 2004

Parent, Mary N., *The Roof in Japanese Buddhist Architecture* (Kajima 1983)

Sadler, A.L., *A Short History of Japanese Architecture* (1962)

Soper, Alexander, *Art and Architecture in China. Part 2: Architecture* (1968)

Soper, Alexander, *The Art and Architecture of Japan. Part 2: Architecture* (2nd edition 1974)

Suzuki, Kakichi, *Early Buddhist Architecture in Japan*, trans. M.N. Parent and N.S. Steinhardt (Kodansha International 1980)

Twitchett, Denis, ed., *The Cambridge History of China. Vol. 3: Sui and T'ang China, 589–906* (Cambridge University Press 1979)

Yiengpruksawan, Mimi Hall, 'The Phoenix Hall at Uji and the Symmetries of Replication', *Art Bulletin*, vol. 77, no. 4 (Dec. 1995), pp. 647–72

Yuenua, Guan, and Zhong Liangbi, trans. and ed., *Behind the Veil of the Forbidden City* (Chinese Literature Press 1996)

Zhuoyun, Yu, *Palaces of the Forbidden City* (Allen Lane 1984)

NORTHERN EUROPE

Affentranger, Christoph, *New Wood Architecture in Scandinavia* (Birkhauser 1997)

Bugge, Gunnar, *Stave Churches in Norway: Introduction and Survey* (Oslo 1983)

Bugge, Gunnar, and Christian Norberg-Schulz, *Stav og Laft: Early Wooden Architecture in Norway* (Oslo 1990)

Derry, T.K., *A History of Scandinavia* (2000)

Erixon, Sigurd, 'The North-European Technique of Corner Timbering', *Folk-Liv*, no. 1 (1937), pp. 13–60

Hauglid, Roar, *Norske Stavkirker* (Oslo 1976)

Hohler, E.B., *Norwegian Stave Church Sculpture* (1999)

Jappinen, Jussi, and Heli-Maija Voutilainen, *The Story of Petajavesi Old Church* (Kopijyva Kustannus, Jyvsasklya 2001)

Jarmund Vigsnæs: ANC Art and Culture (Aug. 2002)

Jones, Gwyn, *A History of the Vikings* (Oxford University Press 1984)

Kavhi, Guthorm, *Norwegian Architecture, Past and Present* (Oslo, 1958)

Menin, S., and F. Samuel, *Nature and Space: Aalto and Le Corbusier* (Routledge 2003)

Norberg-Schulz, Christian, *Modern Norwegian Architecture* (Norwegian University Press 1986)

Pettersson, Lars, *Finnish Wooden Church* (Museum of Finnish Architecture 1989)

Richards, J.M., *800 Years of Finnish Architecture* (Newton Abbott, David and Charles 1978)

Sjostrom, Ingrid, ed., *Kyrka af Trad, Kyrkobyggande under 1600–och 1700 talen, Finland, Norge och Sverlge* (Norsk Institutt for Kulturminneforskning 2000)

Valebrokk, E., and T. Thiis-Evenson, *Norway's Stave Churches. Architecture, History and Legends* (Boksenteret 1994)

WESTERN EUROPE

An Account of the Hospital of Robert Dudley, Earl of Leycester in Warwick (H.T. Cooke & Son, Warwick 1870)

Airs, Malcolm, *The Tudor and Jacobean Country House: A Building History* (Barrie & Jenkins 1982)

Anderegg, J.P., *The Farmhouses of the Canton Freiburg* (1979)

Barber, M, *The New Knighthood; A History of the Order of the Temple* (Cambridge University Press 1994)

Baumgarten, Karl, 'Some Notes on the History of the German Hall House', *Vernacular Architecture*, no. 7 (1979), pp. 15–20

Brandon, Peter, *The Kent and Sussex Weald* (Phillimore & Co 2003)

Brandon, Peter, et al., *Wealden Buildings: Studies in the Timber-Framed Tradition of Building in Kent, Sussex and Surrey: In Tribute to R.T. Mason* (Coach Publishing 1990)

Brown, R.J., *Timber-Framed Buildings of England* (Robert Hale 1986)

Brunskill, Ronald, W., *Traditional Farm Buildings of Britain* (London 1987)

Brunskill, Ronald W., *Timber Building in Britain* (Victor Gollancz 1994)

Clifton-Taylor, Alec, *The Pattern of English Building* (Faber 1972)

Cooper, Nicholas, *Houses of the Gentry, 1480–1680* (Yale University Press 1999)

De L'Orme, Philibert, *Architecture de Philibert de L'Orme* (Pierre Mardaga 1981)

Gibson, Alex, *Stonehenge and Timber Circles* (Tempus Publishing 2000)

Gschwend, M., P. Fehlmann and R. Hunziker, *Ballenberg* (Aarau 1982)

Harris, R., *Discovering Timber-Framed Buildings* (Shire Publications 1978)

Hewitt, Cecil, *English Historic Carpentry* (Phillimore & Co. 1980)

Hewitt, Cecil, *Church Carpentry* (Phillimore & Co. 1982)

Hewitt, Cecil, *English Cathedral and Monastic Carpentry* (Phillimore & Co. 1985)

The Hospital of Robert Dudley Earl of Leycester (Graham Cumming, Ramsgate 1961)

Kirk, Malcolm, *The Barn: Silent Spaces* (Thames & Hudson 1994)

Lord, Evelyn, *The Knights Templar in Britain* (Longman 2004)

Mason, R.T., *Framed Buildings of the Weald* (1969)

Meirion-Jones, Gwyn, 'The Vernacular Architecture of France: An Assessment', *Vernacular Architecture*, vol. 16 (1985)

'Peter Zumthor', *Architecture & Urbanism*, no. 1, 316 (Jan. 1997), pp. 3–91

Pevsner, N., *Shropshire: Buildings of England Series* (Penguin 1975)

Pevsner, N., and A. Wedgwood, *Warwickshire: Buildings of England Series* (Penguin 1966)

Pople, Nic, 'Off the Grid', *RIBA Journal* (May 2002)

Quiney, Anthony, *The Traditional Buildings of England* (Thames & Hudson 1992)

Rackham, O., *The History of the Countryside* (1986)

Rose, W., *The Village Carpenter* (1952)

Runciman, S., *The History of the Crusades* (1968)

Willis, R., and J.W. Clark, *An Architectural History of the University of Cambridge* (Cambridge University Press 1998)

EASTERN EUROPE

Barca, Ana, *Wooden Architecture of Maramures*, trans. James Brown (Humanitas Editura 2001)

Berry, L.E., and R.O. Crummey, eds, *A Rude and Barbarous Kingdom: Russia in the Accounts of 16th-Century English Voyagers* (University of Wisconsin Press 1968)

Brumfield, William C., *A History of Russian Architecture* (Cambridge University Press 1993)

Buxton, David, *The Wooden Churches of Eastern Europe: An Introductory Survey* (Cambridge University Press 1981)

Castellan, A.L., *Lettres sur la Grèce, l'Hellespont et Constantinople* (2 vols, Paris 1811)

Dallaway, James, *Constantinople Ancient and Modern, with Excursions to the Shores and Islands of the Archipelago and to the Troad* (London 1797)

Freely, John, *Istanbul – The Imperial City* (1998)

Gebhard, David, 'The Traditional Wood Houses of Turkey', *AIA Journal* (1963), pp. 36–7

Giurescu, Constantin C., *Transylvania in the History of the Romanian People* (Bucharest 1968)

Giurescu, Constantin C., *A History of the Romanian Forest* (Bucharest 1980)

Goodwin, Godfrey, *A History of Ottoman Architecture* (Thames & Hudson 1971)

Hellier, C., and F. Venturi, *Splendours of the Bosphorus: Houses and Palaces of Istanbul* (Tauris Parke 1993)

Kopp, Anatole, *Town and Revolution: Soviet Architecture and City Planning 1917–1935* (Thames & Hudson 1970)

Kuban, Doğan, *The Turkish Hayat House* (Istanbul 1995)

Opolonikov, A.V., and Y.A. Opolonikov, *The Wooden Architecture of Russia: Houses, Fortifications, Churches* (Thames & Hudson 1989)

Orkinsky, V.P., *Wooden Architecture of Karelia* (Leningrad 1972)

Pardoe, Julia, *The City of the Sultan and Domestic Manners of the Turks in 1836* (London 1837)

Pardoe, Julia, *The Beauties of the Bosphorous* (London 1839)

Patterson, Joby, *Wooden Churches of the Carpathians: A Comparative Study* (Columbia University Press 2001)

Petrescu, Paul, *Wooden Peasant Architecture in Romania* (Bucharest 1974)

AMERICA

Bosley, Edward R., *Greene and Greene* (Phaidon Press 2000)

Bosley, Edward R., *Gamble House: Greene and Greene*, Architecture in Detail series (Phaidon Press 2002)

Connally, E.A., 'The Cape Cod House: An Introductory Survey', *Journal of the Society of Architectural Historians* (May 1960), pp. 47–56

Cummings, Abbott Lowell, *The Fairbanks House: A History of the Oldest Timber-Frame Building in New England* (2002)

Cummings, Abbott Lowell, *The Framed Houses of Massachusetts Bay 1625–1725* (1979)

Downing, A.F., and V.J. Scully, *The Architectural Heritage of Newport, RI, 1640–1915* (Harvard University Press 1952)

Elliott, C.D., *The American Architect from the Colonial Era to the Present* (North Carolina 2003)

Guinness, Desmond, *Newport Preserved: Architecture of the 18th Century* (Viking Press 1982)

Hess, Alan, *Hyperwest – American Residential Architects on the Edge* (Thames & Hudson 1996)

Kornwolf, J.D., *Architecture and Town Planning in Colonial North America* (John Hopkins University Press 2002)

Lassiter, William Lawrence, *Shaker Architecture* (New York, 1966)

McMillen, Elizabeth, *Beach Houses* (Tokyo 1993)

Mead, Christopher Curtis, *The Architecture of Bart Prince* (WW Norton & Co., New York 1999)

Morris, William, *Art and Socialism: A Lecture Delivered Jan. 23 1884 before the Secular Society of Leicester* (W. Reeves, London 1884)

Morrison, Hugh, *Early American Architecture from the First Colonial Settlements to the National Period* (New York 1952)

Mulvagh, J., and M.A. Weber, *Newport Houses* (Rizzoli 1989)

Pearson, C., ed., *Modern American Houses* (Abrams, 1996)

Robbins, W.G., *Lumberjacks and Legislators: Political Economy of the US Lumber Industry 1890–1941* (Texas 1982)

Roth, Leland M., *McKim, Mead and White, Architects* (Thames & Hudson 1984)

Roth, Leland M., and B. Morgan, *Shingle Styles: Innovation and Tradition in American Architecture* (Harry N. Abrams 1999)

Scully, Vincent J., *The Shingle Style and the Stick Style: Architectural Theory and Design from Richardson to the Origins of Wright* (Yale University Press 1955)

Scully, Vincent J., *The Architecture of the American Summer – The Flowering of the Shingle Style* (Rizzoli 1989)

Stein, Stephen J., *The Shaker Experience in America: A History of the United Society of Believers* (Yale University Press 1992)

Webb, Michael, 'Architecture Twist and Shout', *Architectural Digest* (Oct. 1997)

Whiffen, M., and F. Koeper, *American Architecture 1607–1976* (MIT 1981)

White, S.G., *The Houses of McKim, Mead and White* (Thames & Hudson 1998)

Woodbridge, Sally B., *California Architecture: Historic American Buildings Survey* (Chronicle Books 1988)

SOUTH-EAST ASIA

Aasen, Clarence, *The Architecture of Siam: A Cultural History Interpretation* (Oxford University Press 1998)

Bernet Kempers, A.J., *Ancient Indonesian Art* (1959)

Bernet Kempers, A.J., *Monumental Bali* (Van Goer Zonen, The Hague 1990)

Buchanan, B.S., *Burmese Traditions* (London 1932)

Chaichongrak, Ruethai, Somchai Nil-athi and Ornsiri Panin, *The Thai House: History and Evolution* (River Books 2002)

Dawson, Barry, and John Gillow, *The Traditional Architecture of Indonesia* (Thames & Hudson 1994)

Dumarcay, Jacques, *Mission Report March/April 1983* (UN Report on Burmese Monasteries 1983)

Eisemann, Fred B., *Bali: Sekala and Niskala Vols 1 and 2* (Periplus Editions 1990)

Fergusson, James, *History of Indian and Eastern Architecture* (London 1876)

Fraser-Lu, Sylvia, *Splendour in Wood: The Buddhist Monasteries of Burma* (Orchid Press, Bangkok 2001)

Freeman, Michael, *Lanna: Thailand's Northern Kingdom* (Thames & Hudson, London 2001)

Green, A., and T.R. Blurton, eds, *Burma: Art and Archaeology* (British Museum Press 2002)

Hyde, Richard, 'Jim Thompson's House: Traditional Thai Housing Adapted', *Open House International*, vol. 11, no. 1 (1986)

Jumsai, Sumet, *Architectural Forms of Northern Siam and Old Siamese Fortifications* (Bangkok 1970)

Lehman, F.K., 'Monasteries, Palaces and Ambiguities: Burmese Sacred and Secular Space', *Contributions to Indian Sociology*, vol. 21, no. 1 (1987)

Le May, R., *A Concise History of Buddhist Art in Siam* (1938)

Rawson, Philip, *The Art of South East Asia* (Thames & Hudson 1967)

Rodger, Alex, *A Handbook of the Forest Products of Burma* (Rangoon, 1936)

Silpa, Bhirasri, *Thai Buddhist Art* (5th edition, The Fine Arts Department, Bangkok 1979)

Tun, Than, *Essays on the History and Buddhism of Burma*, ed. Paul Strachen (Kiscadale Publications 1988)

Van Beek, S., and L.I. Tettoni, *An Introduction to the Arts of Thailand* (Hong Kong 1985)

Warren, William, *The House on the Klong: The Bangkok Home and Asian Art Collection of James Thompson* (Weatherhill, New York 1968)

Wyatt, D., *Thailand: A Short History* (Yale University Press 1984)

AUSTRALIA

Andrews, Brian, *Australian Gothic: The Gothic Revival in Australian Architecture from the 1840s to the 1950s* (Melbourne University Press 2001)

Baker, Richard, *The Hardwoods of Australia and their Economics* (Sydney 1919)

Bingham-Hall, Patrick, *A Short History of Brisbane Architecture* (Pesaro Publishing, Sydney 2001)

Bingham-Hall, Patrick, *A Short History of Melbourne Architecture* (Pesaro Publishing, Sydney 2001)

Bell, Peter, 'Square Timber Boxes on Long Legs – Timber Houses in North Queensland', *Historic Environment* 6 (1988), pp. 32–7

Bootle, Keith R., *Wood in Australia: Types, Properties and Uses* (Sydney Book Company 1983)

Boyd, R., *Australia's Home: Its Origins, Builders and Occupiers* (Melbourne 1952)

Clark, Manning, *A Short History of Australia* (1992)

Cox, P., J.M. Freeland and W. Stacey, *Rude Timber Buildings in Australia* (Thames & Hudson 1969)

Cox, Philip, and David Moore, *The Australian Functional Tradition* (1988)

De Grauchy, Graham, *Architecture in Brisbane* (1988)

Evans, I., *The Federation House* (1986)

Fisher, Rod, and Brian Crozier, eds, *The Queensland House: A Roof over our Heads* (Queensland Museum 1994)

Francis, W.D., *Australian Rain-forest Trees* (Sydney 1951)

Goad and Place, *A Short History of Melbourne Architecture* (2002)

Howells, Trevor, and Michael Nicholson, *Towards the Dawn: Federation Architecture in Australia 1890–1915* (1989)

Irving, Robert, *The History and Design of the Australian House* (Oxford University Press 1985)

Macintyre, Stuart, *A Concise History of Australia* (Cambridge University Press 1999)

Macmahon, Bill, *The Architecture of East Australia* (2001)

Martin, Ged, *The Founding of Australia: The Argument about Australia's Origins* (Sydney 1978)

Saini, B.S., *Architecture in Tropical Queensland* (Melbourne University Press 1970)

Smith, Robin, *Australia's Eucalypts* (Melbourne 1980)

Tanner, Howard, ed., *Architects of Australia* (Macmillan, Melbourne 1981)

Watson, Donald, *The Queensland House* (1981)

Wood in Culture Association, *Richard Leplastrier: Spirit of Nature Wood Architecture Award 2004* (Tampere, Finland 2004)

GENERAL

Blaser, Werner, *Fantasy in Wood: Elements of Architectural Style c.1900* (Birkhauser Verlag AG 1987)

Hansen, H.J., ed., *Architecture in Wood: A History of Wood Building and its Techniques in Europe and North America*, trans. Janet Seligman (Faber & Faber 1971)

Hagan, Susannah, 'Five Reasons to Adopt Environmental Design', *Harvard Design Magazine*, no. 18 (spring/summer 2003)

Hayman, Richard, *Trees: Woodland and Western Civilisation* (2003)

Kuchli, Christian, *Forests of Hope* (Earthscan 1997)

Lefaivre, L., A. Tzonis and B. Stagno, *Tropical Architecture: Critical Regionalism in the Age of Globalization* (Wiley-Academy 2001)

Lomberg, Bjorn, *The Skeptical Environmentalist: Measuring the Real State of the World* (Cambridge University Press 1998)

Marland, G., *The Prospect of Solving the CO_2 Problem through Global Reforestation* (US Department of Energy 1988)

MCPFE Liaison Unit & UNECE/FAO, *State of Europe's Forests 2003* (Ministerial Conference on the Protection of Forests in Europe 2003)

Oliver, Paul, *Shelter and Society: New Studies in Vernacular Architecture* (Barrie & Jenkins 1970)

Oliver, Paul, ed., *Encyclopedia of Vernacular Architecture of the World* (Cambridge University Press 1998)

Oliver, Paul, *Dwellings: The Vernacular House World Wide* (Phaidon Press 2003)

Schittich, Christian, 'Modern Timber Construction', *Detail*, no. 5 (2002)

Stungo, Naomi, *The New Wood Architecture* (Laurence King, London 1998)

Turner, Jane, ed., *The Grove Dictionary of Art* (Oxford University Press 2003)

Vale, Brenda, and Robert Vale, *Towards a Green Architecture* (RIBA Publications 1991)

Vitruvius, *Ten Books on Architecture*, trans. Ingrid Rowland (Cambridge University Press 1999)

Willis, Anne-Marie, and Cameron Tonkin, *Timber in Context: A Guide to Sustainable Use* (1998)

Wines, James, *Green Architecture* (Taschen 2000)

Zwerger, Klaus, *Wood and Wood Joints: Building Traditions of Europe and Japan* (Birkhauser, Basel 1997)

ACKNOWLEDGMENTS

Thanks to: Julie Aalen of the Weald & Downland Museum; Andrew Abbott; Brit Andresen; the Ballenberg Museum, Switzerland; Tom Bjørnstad; Marcus Bleasdale; Anna Blomefield; Eric Booth; Hilde Chapman of the Norwegian Embassy in London; Kylie Clark of the Japan National Tourist Organization; Natasha Glushkoff of the Haas-Lilenthal House; Kristen Grieg Bjerke of Fortidsmineforenigen (The Society for the Preservation of Cultural Heritage, Oslo); John Hardy; Einar Jarmund; Maurice Jennings; David Kohn; C.Y. Kuan; Rick Leplastrier; Lt-Col. Gerald Lesinski of Lord Leycester's Hospital; Julie Letendre of the Fairbanks House; Linda MacLachlan & Martin Harris; Bobbi Mapstone of the Gamble House; Yoko Matsumura; Sally Morse Majewski of Hancock Shaker Village; Joe Price; Bart Prince; Ingela Qvarfot of Skansen Museum, Stockholm; Oddbjørn Sørmoen of Riksantikvaren; Mirja Räty of Petajavesi Old Church; William C.S. Remsen; Skaaheim Rikvald of Gardermoen Airport; Charles Trevor; John Tschirch & Andrea Carneiro of the Newport Historical Society; Jeremy Vibert; the Vitoslavlitsy Museum, Novgorod; and Christopher Wright. Also thanks to numerous monks, church keyholders and caretakers for access to many of the lesser-known buildings.

Also thanks to my travel agents Sam Davies & Tim Jones of Trailfinders; and Melonie Simons of Adventure Overland.

Particular thanks are due to James W.P. Campbell, Jonathan Sachs and the patient staff at Thames & Hudson. Many thanks are also due to Susan Olle for her exceptional skill and dedication.

Many thanks to the following organizations for their generous support of this project: TRADA; Wood for Good.

And thanks to those friends who very kindly gave me hospitality around the world: Andrew & Lorna Camden; Anthony & Lilly Camden; Pamela Druckerman & Simon Kuper; Robert & Isobel Gotto; Deanna Griffin; Ophelia Field & Paul Laikin; Philip & Julie Lewin; Michelle Manz; K.B. Nøsterud; Peggy & Michael Strong; Shona & Mark Van Lieshout; Adrian & Teresa Richardson (& Mr. Li); and Frank Wuest.

For everything else, thanks to Colette.